The Battle of Ideas in the War on Terror

Essays on U.S. Public Diplomacy in the Middle East

Robert Satloff

The Washington Institute for Near East Policy

Published in 2004 in the United States of America by The Washington Institute for Near East Policy, 1828 L Street NW, Suite 1050, Washington, DC 20036.

Library of Congress Cataloging-in-Publication Data

Satloff, Robert
    The battle of ideas in the war on terror : essays on U.S. public diplomacy in the Middle East / by Robert Satloff.
    p. cm.
    ISBN 0-944029-92-2
    1. United States—Relations—Arab countries. 2. Arab countries—Relations—United States. 3. War on Terrorism, 2001—Public opinion. 4. Public opinion—Arab countries. 5. United States—Foreign public opinion, Arab. 6. Public relations and politics—United States. 7. Public relations and politics—Arab countries. I. Title.

DS63.2.U5S26 2004
327.73056'09'0511—dc22

2004021790

Design by Daniel Kohan, Sensical Design & Communication
Front cover photo: Pupil in a Palestinian classroom, 1993. © Peter Turnley/CORBIS

The Author

R OBERT SATLOFF RESUMED HIS POST AS EXECUTIVE director of The Washington Institute for Near East Policy in July 2004 after more than two years living in Morocco. He first assumed the directorship in January 1993.

Before and during his stay in Morocco, Dr. Satloff traveled widely throughout the Middle East, writing extensively on ways to fix America's troubled public diplomacy toward Arabs and Muslims. In addition, his personal research overseas focused on unearthing stories of Arab "heroes" and "villains" of the Holocaust, drawing on archives, interviews, and site visits in eleven countries.

Dr. Satloff is author or editor of nine books, monographs, and collected volumes on Arab and Islamic politics, the Arab-Israeli peace process, and U.S. Middle East policy. His commentary on a wide variety of Middle East issues has appeared in various media outlets—television, radio, and print—throughout the United States and abroad.

Dr. Satloff received his doctorate in Oriental Studies (Modern Middle Eastern History) from St. Antony's College, Oxford University.

Table of Contents

Acknowledgments

T HE UNDERLYING PREMISE OF THIS COLLECTION OF ESSAYS is that ideas matter. But a set of ideas does not emerge either all at once or all by itself. This volume represents not only a compilation of essays I have written on public diplomacy since the aftermath of the September 11 attacks, but also the evolution of my thinking on that topic. While the final products are mine alone, many people helped me see the potential for America's engagement with Middle Easterners in new and different ways.

First, I owe a deep debt to my colleagues at The Washington Institute—permanent senior research staff, visiting fellows, associate scholars, and research assistants—who discussed and debated many of these ideas with me over the years. Each is an expert in his or her field; collectively, they form a creative and congenial research team that is even more potent than the sum of its parts. I am especially grateful to Dennis Ross, who served as director of the Institute during my overseas absence with characteristic good humor and sound judgment, and to Patrick Clawson, Institute deputy director, who ably rose to the task of managing the organization's day-to-day operations during that time. Special thanks are also due to publications director Alicia Gansz and publications associate George Lopez, committed professionals in all respects; to David Makovsky, whose intellectual and logistical contributions made possible a group interview with Arab liberals in September 2003; to Martin Schneider, dollar-for-dollar one of the finest research assistants anyone could hope for; and to Marguerite Hellwich, my inestimable executive assistant.

Second, a number of friends and colleagues have been instrumental in shaping my views of the Middle East and, especially, the role and importance of public diplomacy. Martin Kramer, David Pollock, Helena Kane

Finn, Alan Makovsky, and Amy Hawthorne each played an invaluable role in my education on the subject. Adam Garfinkle gave me the opportunity to test new ideas in an excellent and provocative volume that he edited. Mouafac Harb has done his best to prove, on a daily basis, that the U.S. government might actually be capable of broadcasting effectively to Arabs. And Bernard Lewis, in writing and in person, has never failed to provide new insights into old problems and advance warning of new problems.

Third, this volume itself owes its existence to a suggestion made during one of scores of telephone calls I have held over the years with Barbi Weinberg, Mike Stein, and Fred Lafer. These three wise, selfless, and generous people have provided The Washington Institute with guidance and leadership for nearly two decades. During much of this period, they also provided me with a level of support and confidence that should be the envy of all, especially as they braved my decision to move abroad in 2002.

Fourth, over the past three years, I received advice, support, and information from many active and retired U.S. government officials with expertise in either public diplomacy or Middle East affairs. While most prefer to remain anonymous, I break no confidences in praising their consistent and consummate professionalism. I have also benefited from the interest in public diplomacy issues exhibited by policymakers and political leaders at all levels of the U.S. government, many of whom took the time to listen patiently to my critiques and proposals. At a time of armed conflict on multiple fronts, recognizing the importance of the battle of ideas is a mark of vision. I am particularly grateful to Congressmen Howard Berman (D-Calif.) and Joseph Knollenberg (R-Mich.), who cosponsored the American School Abroad Support Act (HR 4303), an idea that grew out of my family's richly rewarding experience at the Rabat American School.

Fifth, special thanks are due to the many Arabs and other Middle Easterners I met during my travels, my research, and my time living in Morocco. Although the essays in this collection span only the past three years, they represent the distillation of twenty years of personal engagement with the peoples of the Middle East. Along the way, I benefited immensely from the openness, candor, and graciousness of dozens of people from all walks of life and all strata of society. Some became good friends; others were passing acquaintances who left an indelible mark. To name any might cause unnecessary embarrassment, but I owe them all my gratitude.

Last, and most important, I am deeply grateful to my family. If the underlying message in this volume is one of hope and optimism, it is due largely to the happy experience of sharing countless moments of adventure and discovery with my wife, Jennie, and our two children, Benjamin and William, during our twenty-seven months in Morocco. To view Arabs, the Middle East, and the world through their eyes, not just mine, is to see it anew, which is a blessing indeed.

Robert Satloff
Washington, D.C.
October 2004

Introduction

EVEN BEFORE THE FLAMES RAGING WITHIN THE TWISTED steel of the fallen World Trade Center towers were extinguished, a debate began to flare up regarding the motivations of the perpetrators. How could Arab Muslim society produce young, well-educated men filled with such hatred toward America that they would kill more than 3,000 innocents—as well as themselves—to prove a point? Some argued that the killers were representative of a strain of Muslim revulsion at "who we are"—that is, a profound hatred of American values, culture, and society. Others argued that disgust over "what we do"—U.S. policy regarding Israel, oil, Arab autocrats, and Islam itself—was the main source of the animus. Advocates of each position had their policy prescriptions readily at hand. The latter argued that we should change our policy to reduce the level of disgust among Arabs and Muslims. The former suggested nothing but staying the course, arguing that military victory alone would alter the calculus of hatred. This collection of essays owes its origin to my dissatisfaction with both sets of recommendations for U.S. policy.

A relatively small but still sizable, intensely ambitious, and disproportionately powerful subgroup of Muslims do indeed hate "who we are." For the most part, these are Islamists—Muslims who reject modern notions of state, citizen, and individual rights and instead seek to impose a totalitarian version of Islam on peoples and nations around the globe. Within this subgroup are those who seek power through revolutionary or violent means and others who seek it through evolutionary or nonviolent means. While the former are unabashed terrorists, it is equally true that the latter can never be democrats.

There are also many Muslims who, while not Islamists, are genuinely angered by certain U.S. policies abroad. U.S. policy analysts would be doing their country a disservice by not recognizing this fact. While the outrage expressed by these Muslims may be episodic and almost surely lacks the operational significance often ascribed to it, it is nonetheless real and cannot merely be wished away by changing the topic.

And, lest we forget, there is a large percentage of Muslims whose daily lives are not animated by any of these issues. These are the tens of millions whose energies are completely sapped by the uphill struggle to eke out a living. They might have some passing knowledge of goings-on in faraway Baghdad or Gaza and may, if asked, express an opinion on them. But their interests and concerns are consumed by more urgent demands.

Regarding the various stripes of Islamists, the United States can do nothing to soften their hearts or change their minds. The goal of U.S. policy should instead be to seek their defeat—through military means for those who use violence to gain power, and through political means for those whose tactics take a more circuitous path to the same objective. There is no benefit to be gained from targeting public diplomacy toward the Islamists.

Regarding other Muslims who actively critique U.S. policy, there is much the United States can do apart from the obviously self-defeating approach of changing policies to appease the critics. Given the structural biases, shoddy journalism, and intellectual drivel that passes for political discourse in many corners of the Middle East, America's top priority vis-à-vis these Muslims should be to make sure that their opinions are at least based on accurate, dispassionate information. In this regard, public diplomacy can help to create a "level playing field" so that U.S. policies (and the people advocating them) receive a fair hearing in the court of public opinion. Numerous tactical options flow from this strategy.

And regarding the millions of poor and struggling Muslims, the goal of U.S. policy should be to help provide them with the economic, educational, social, and other tools required to leave poverty behind and become constructive and contributing members of their societies. A wide range of policy instruments are available to achieve this goal, complemented by public diplomacy that underscores America's concern and commitment on a personal level.

The story does not end there, however. The key ingredient missing from most analyses of the "why do they hate us?" problem is a recognition that the first two groups of Muslims—those whose hatred arises from "who we are" and those whose critique is based on "what we do"—are also battling each other over the fate and direction of their societies. On rare occasions—Algeria in the 1990s, for example—this battle has devolved into a shooting war. More commonly, it is a battle of ideas over how to organize societies. The fact that this battle rages in most countries without too many bombs going off or too many dead bodies piling up neither renders it any less momentous nor makes the imperative of victory any less urgent.

The United States has a vital stake in the outcome of this battle, both for the sake of Muslims themselves and for the security of Americans and U.S. interests in Arab and Muslim countries. Without reservation or apology, America's strategy should be to help non- and anti-Islamist Muslims beat back the Islamist challenge. This strategy must be pursued even if many of these putative Muslim allies express bitter dislike for certain aspects of U.S. foreign policy.

In the post–September 11 era, public diplomacy should be focused on fighting the battle of ideas in Muslim societies. This is a battle that can be won, though it will take more time, money, commitment, and ingenuity than the U.S. government has so far been willing to dedicate to the task.

This set of essays discusses the many problems plaguing public diplomacy in the post–September 11 era and proposes how the United States should pursue what many regard as a mission impossible. Collectively, the essays span the three years since September 11. Four of them were written expressly for this collection, while the balance appeared previously in various publications and are reprinted here as originally published.

There are distinct advantages to using this format. A series of brief essays on discrete subtopics, written and developed over time, both makes the subjects discussed more accessible and provides a chronological context to evolving debates over public diplomacy. This approach may mean that some issues appear fresher and seem to merit more detailed discussion than others. Hopefully, that problem is outweighed by the benefits of following the intellectual odyssey that I undertook as I focused on the public diplomacy challenges facing America since September 11.

Seven months after the al-Qaeda attacks in the United States, my family and I moved from Washington to Rabat, Morocco, capital of a populous Arab Muslim country located at a strategic point between the Atlantic and the Mediterranean, just nine miles from Europe. We lived in Rabat for more than two years, during a time of great challenge and turbulence. We traveled to every corner of the country and met Moroccans from all walks of life. I traveled to many corners of the Middle East as well. My wife and I learned much through our children and their experiences; one of our sons attended an outstanding local Moroccan school, while another attended the Rabat American School, an institution that provides the finest of American-style education to a student body that is overwhelmingly non-American. And, not being American officials ourselves, we were free to explore certain places at certain times when our diplomat friends did not have this license, such as when the entire family drove to downtown Rabat to witness one of the largest anti–Iraq war protests in the Middle East.

My summary assessment—that the battle of ideas can be won if the United States is willing to commit itself to helping its current and potential Muslim allies "fight the fight"—emerges in large part from my experience abroad. While this theme is present in several of the early essays in this collection, it is expounded with increasing confidence and buoyancy over time. Without minimizing the daunting obstacles that lie ahead, I am convinced that a public diplomacy infused with hope, optimism, candor, creativity, resources, and an entrepreneurial approach to building and supporting allies is the right strategy for America in the Middle East.

PART I

A Strategy for Public Diplomacy

Devising a Public Diplomacy Campaign toward the Middle East: Part I—Basic Principles

October 2001

T HE APPEARANCE OF SENIOR U.S. OFFICIALS ON THE Qatari-based al-Jazeera satellite news channel is the first sign that Washington is taking seriously the need for enhanced "public diplomacy" as a vital component in the war against terrorism. In this arena, however, urgency needs to be tempered with realism. Rushing to enhance public diplomacy efforts without a clear understanding of objectives, constraints, sequence, and the different means at the government's disposal risks not only a dispersal of effort and wasted resources but, in the worst case, actually ceding important ground in the "hearts-and-minds" campaign. In devising public diplomacy toward the Middle East, the key to success will be to marry the principles of "make haste, slowly" and "do no harm."

Objective

In general, a public diplomacy campaign waged in the current political context ought to have three basic components:

1. Explaining U.S. policy, candidly and without apology. America has a strong, positive record on issues of concern to Arabs and Muslims and should make its case. Washington should be justifiably proud of its military efforts to defend Muslim populations in Bosnia, Kosovo, and Kuwait; the health, welfare, and infrastructure improvements purchased by the tens of billions of dollars of assistance to the largest Arab state, Egypt; and the mutually benefi-

---

Originally published as *PolicyWatch* number 579, October 30, 2001.

cial relations it has with governments from Nigeria to Turkey to Indonesia. Similarly, the United States should not shy away from explaining its support for Israel and its generation-old effort to promote a peaceful, negotiated settlement of the Arab-Israeli dispute, nor should it flinch from highlighting the ongoing threat that Saddam Husayn poses to his people and the wider region and the need to maintain tight constraints on Saddam's ability to act on his oft-stated ambitions.

2. Providing alternative sources of credible, factual, relevant information, especially about the wider world but also about the local countries in which listeners and viewers live. Rather than seek to compete with the sensationalism that characterizes Arab satellite television stations, U.S.-produced news should be presented in a professional and dispassionate manner, but one that highlights free and open debate among responsible political elements. For reasons outlined below, programming should be country-specific, as much as possible.

3. Projecting those core U.S. values that characterize U.S. society, especially tolerance, openness, meritocracy, and civic activism. This is a much more modest objective than aspiring to enlist popular support for U.S. policy throughout Arab and Muslim societies or to build future pro-American governments in the region. The objective here should be to expose Middle Easterners to information about the American way of life and to provide local populations with a choice about how they wish to develop their own societies, not that the United States is going to impose that choice on them. While the United States cannot award every Middle Easterner a visa, U.S. public diplomacy can give every reader, listener, and viewer a portal into the American way of life, providing them with an opportunity to learn that functioning, flourishing alternatives exist to their generally closed and illiberal societies.

Context

The first step in devising a public diplomacy campaign to complement the "war on terror" is to recognize the complexity of the challenge; the distinction between target-states and target-peoples; and fundamental differences between the current situation and the U.S.-Soviet ideological struggle of years past.

- The targets in the current situation are populations of states whose governments range from those that are, more or less, supportive of U.S. security interests (e.g., Egypt, Saudi Arabia) to those that are inimical to our interests (e.g., Syria, Iran).

- In terms of public diplomacy, the distinction between allies and adversaries is blurred. Both friendly and unfriendly states alike fend off domestic criticism of internal problems by offering wide latitude to anti-Americanism in all spheres of public discourse, especially media, culture, religion, and education. While this does not obviate the very real problem of animosity to U.S. policy in many corners of the Middle East, this does mean that U.S. public diplomacy will face an uphill battle in almost every Middle Eastern state.

- In general, civil society organizations that, in other cultures and at other times, might be ready partners for U.S. public diplomacy either cannot or will not play that role in the current Middle East context. Some are Islamist in orientation and are avowedly anti-American. Many others, especially those involved in local health and welfare service delivery, are predominantly nonpolitical and must remain that way to avoid running afoul of the regime. Sadly, to the extent that they exist, the Walensas, Sharanskys, and Havels of the Middle East are not generally friendly to U.S. Middle East policy. Ironically, those most naturally sympathetic to the United States may be found in organizations connected to, though not directly part of, the regime, as well as in the business communities; however, these organizations are also likely to make a distinction between U.S. values (which they appreciate) and U.S. policies (which they oppose). The bottom line is that organized civil society will not be a strong ally in this effort, though a handful of groups may support specific initiatives and deserve U.S. engagement.

Taken together, all this suggests the need for extreme humility in devising a public diplomacy campaign targeted toward the states and peoples in the Middle East. Thankfully, this region of the world is less critical to current U.S. military operations than was the case with the Gulf War a decade ago; today, the key Muslim-majority states in terms of the U.S. military effort are Pakistan and Uzbekistan, not Egypt and Saudi Arabia. Nevertheless, the Arab Middle East still needs to be a central concern because of other current

U.S. interests and because the campaign against terror may before long turn its focus here. At the same time, as one pundit has noted, this part of the globe is undergoing a "clash within civilization," which any U.S. outreach effort can affect only on the margins and only over time.

Four immediate policy consequences emerge from the above:

1. The state-supported anti-Americanism of existing media/religious/educational elite institutions throughout the region means that any public diplomacy effort begins with the White House. Unless bilateral diplomacy addresses this issue at the highest levels—that is, unless the president and his senior aides are willing to raise with leaders of Egypt and other states the need to purge state-run media of its rampant anti-Americanism (and anti-Semitism), the need for the leaders themselves to adopt clear public stands against these noxious trends, and the need for friendly regimes to lower the vast array of bureaucratic barriers they place in the way of U.S. engagement with local NGOs and ordinary people—then there is little chance that America's own public diplomacy campaign will register much success.

2. As much as possible, efforts at public diplomacy under the broad rubric of "Arab world" or "Muslim world" should be rejected in favor of country-specific initiatives. This flows from the fact that a key subtext of U.S. regional strategy should be to avoid feeding into transnational tides of pan-Arabism or pan-Islamism in favor of evolutionary political and economic change within existing state structures and national borders. On a practical level, it is important to recognize how diverse the Middle East actually is and, for example, to avoid lumping together the vastly different cultures and societies of Casablanca, Aleppo, Muscat, and Riyadh under the simplistic category of "Arab" or "Muslim."

3. Focusing on individual states, however, will pose its own set of problems. The difficulty of directing regime-specific messages (except via national "surrogate radio stations" like Radio Free Iraq) will perforce dictate a lowest-common-denominator form of public diplomacy throughout the region, so as not to provoke insurrectionary sentiment in countries where it could backfire against U.S. interests. Even so, the administration is still going to face stiff opposition, primarily from "friendly regimes" who are likely to view an enhanced public diplomacy effort as meddlesome interference in local affairs.

4. The paucity of local partners, even in countries with significant civil society institutions (such as Morocco, Iran, or the Palestinian Authority) will reinforce the need to focus both on broad target groups (e.g., youth, women) and on themes which appear non-threatening but which have significant political content in the long run (e.g., education, community action, and tolerance).

In general, those devising a U.S. public diplomacy campaign targeted to Arab and Muslim-majority states (as well as to Muslim minorities elsewhere) should avoid two themes:

1. That Americans (even American Muslims) know Islam better than other Muslims do. It makes little sense for U.S. political leaders to preach to Middle Eastern Muslims that Osama bin Laden does not represent "true Islam." That message will resonate only if broadcast by moderate Muslim clerics within the societies in which listeners/viewers live. U.S. diplomacy should actively engage with local religious leaders to convince them (or cajole local political leaders to convince their own local religious leaders) to issue clear statements against extremism and violence, which will be much more powerful than protestations about Islam by U.S. politicians. (It is essential that such condemnations not be limited to the events of September 11; to be lasting and powerful, they should address all terrorism—that is, all attacks on civilians, regardless of political context or alleged objective.) The more appropriate role for American Muslims in U.S. public diplomacy is to advertise the religious tolerance of U.S. society and the freedom within America to debate U.S. policy.

2. That America is keen to understand why so many in the region "hate us." While journalists are keen to hype the anti-Americanism of local populations, it is both self-defeating and analytically unproven to assume that large majorities in the Arab and/or Muslim worlds detest the United States. That many, probably most, Middle Easterners are critical of specific U.S. policies is neither new nor a surprise, given America's status as the sole superpower, arbiter of global culture, and engine of a globalization process in which the Middle East participates only marginally. At the same time, as the small but vocal and politically active class is avowedly anti-American, the large "silent majority" of Arabs and Muslims most likely relishes the idea of coming to America, knows little about the reality of American life, and is exposed only to the caricature of U.S. policies they see on local media. In short, there is a difference between opposition and hate, and to the extent they hate, they hate a phantom.

Exacerbating the challenge for U.S. policymakers is the fact that the most obvious and logical resource for public diplomacy to the Middle East—that is, the professional class of U.S. experts on contemporary Middle East politics and society—is generally (though not uniformly) hostile to U.S. Middle East policy. Most would cause more mischief than good should they be entrusted with creating and implementing a public diplomacy campaign. As a rule, seeking out scholars and policy practitioners who can provide a robust explanation of U.S. policy, even if they are not necessarily "Middle East experts," should be a higher priority than putting on display for Middle Easterners the diversity of U.S. views that is a hallmark of our democracy.

Devising a Public Diplomacy Campaign toward the Middle East: Part II—Core Elements

October 2001

THERE ARE THREE BASIC ELEMENTS OF AN INTEGRATED public diplomacy campaign—media, education, and exchange. More needs to be done in each arena. But before the government falls prey to the appeal of waging "information warfare" via the airwaves as the main way to complement the military campaign now underway, it would be wise to invest in three areas first: making America's diplomats take seriously the goal of public outreach abroad and mandating the language requirements to make that possible; restoring funding and urgency to educational and exchange programs of proven success; and developing ways to engage the next generation of Middle Easterners, especially through English education and American studies programming. After all, the battle for hearts and minds, like the war on terror, is a long-term project.

Media

The easiest target for enhanced public diplomacy is broadcasting—that is, television and radio—but this is also the most delicate, difficult, and, potentially, the most problematic. In a perfect world, the U.S. government would compete for Middle Eastern listeners and viewers with its own network of powerful FM radio stations and satellite television channels that wins audience by appealing to the current tastes of Arabic-, Persian-, and Turkish-speaking Generation Xers and then provides educational, informational, cultural, and entertainment programming that expands minds and wins hearts.

Originally published as *PolicyWatch* number 580, October 31, 2001.

Regrettably, this is precisely what the U.S. government is ill suited to do. While the United States has a strong, if uneven, record in terms of surrogate radio to adversary states, broadcasting to strategically friendly but politically ambiguous states is much more difficult. Success would require a news organization as well-heeled, fleet-footed, and hi-tech as al-Jazeera, trying to win the sort of credibility that it took the BBC decades to acquire.

One obvious impediment will be personnel and oversight. Done properly, pro-U.S. radio and television would require hiring scores of Arab journalists and technicians to maintain local bureaus in many Arab and Muslim countries, providing the raw material for the local news and features that would give U.S. broadcasting its unique appeal. This runs two types of risks: either that the correspondents "go local" and fail to project adequately the pro-U.S. message that is the rationale for the station, or that they (and their families) find themselves subject to enormous pressure—both directly and indirectly, overt and subtle—from local governments or nongovernmental political groups. (The pressure would be magnified in the event that U.S. radio or television tries to establish full-scale broadcast centers in the Middle East, as was the original intent of the new Middle East Radio Network soon to be launched by the Broadcasting Board of Governors.) In either case, finding and keeping the proper balance, without either subjecting staff to life-threatening situations or provoking the ire of Congress when broadcasts are not sufficiently pro-American, is a herculean task.

In the near term, it is important to enhance existing Voice of America programming to the Middle East and to proceed with the BBG's new radio initiative—under careful and ongoing supervision—so as to test the practicability of the concept. But it is at least as important and no less urgent to pursue lower-profile, lower-cost, less labor-intensive media work that is likely to provide more lasting "bang" for the public diplomacy "buck." This means building on opportunities—people, programs, and technology—that already exist. Operationally, this includes:

- **Providing career incentives for local diplomats, especially ambassadors, to do television, radio, and media outreach.** Currently, the incentive structure works the wrong way, as ambassadors and other diplomats can get in trouble if they stray from anodyne State Department guidance but score few career points if they make media outreach a major focus. Instead, the State Department should borrow from the Pentagon model, legislated in the Goldwater-Nichols military reform act, that required officers with "joint" service to be promoted at least as fast as those without, thereby making "joint" service a career-enhancer rather than a dead end. In this context, the State Department should implement (perhaps as a result of new legislation) new policies making good performance at appearing on local media a major factor in the promotion process.

- **Regularizing the appearance of senior government officials on major foreign media.** While the U.S. government should be modest about developing its own satellite television capability, it should assiduously take advantage of the scores of Middle East journalists—print and electronic—eager to air and publish the comments of U.S. officials. With a well-run public diplomacy program, appearances on regional broadcasting by the secretary of state and the national security advisor will be as routine as their appearance on Sunday morning network talk shows. Also, funding should be found to provide media training—by both U.S. professionals and local experts—to U.S. diplomats in the field.

- **Improving language skills of foreign service officers.** The best public diplomacy efforts will fail if diplomats abroad lack language skills to relate to local media and, more generally, to engage ordinary people. In current practice, there is little incentive or support for improving language skills above a 3.0 rating, which is adequate for conversation but not for television or radio appearances. A target goal should be to improve the language skills of 10 percent of FSOs to a 4.0 or higher. This would require additional funds for training facilities and teachers, the time for FSOs to spend upgrading their skills, and the salary incentives to encourage language expertise, especially in strategically important languages like Arabic, Persian, Chinese, and the Turkic family of languages.

- **Funding programs and staff to restore or expand local-language magazines, translation programs, websites, and e-zines, whose budgets have been cut or lost ground to inflation in recent years.** A key area is to expand programs to provide both original and translated articles to local and regional newspapers. (A State Department official recently confided that if five major Arabic newspapers or newsweeklies offered the U.S. government an "American page" to fill as it sees fit, it would take a year before any printable copy could be produced, given existing staffing and responsibilities.) In general, the decision to sacrifice printed materials to push internet-based programming was a mistake, given that the Middle East is one of the world's least-linked parts of the world. Middle Easterners read, and the written message—in contrast to broadcasting—can be recycled for multiple users.

Education

Curiously, thousands of U.S. students may study in Middle Eastern studies programs at the undergraduate and graduate level, but remarkably few Middle Eastern students study in American studies programs. In fact, the first graduate-level, certificate-granting program in American studies was just established in September 2000, at the University of Jordan in Amman. Individual courses exist here and there—primarily at elite schools like the American Universities of Cairo and Beirut, often taught by traveling Fulbright scholars—and a small number of U.S. universities are working to set up local branches or specialized professional schools. But despite these modest programs, the sad fact is that the vast majority of Arab university students have no opportunity to learn about American government, politics, society, or culture. (The U.S. government, for example, has never had an educational partnership grant linked to a Gulf state.) And the situation is, perhaps, even worse for the tens of millions of Middle Easterners in primary or secondary school.

That the people of the Middle East understand better how U.S. society works should be critically important to U.S. public diplomacy. Two priorities should be to promote such programs at major Middle East universities and to establish new avenues for cooperation with local educators to inject American studies modules into primary and secondary education. The U.S. government should begin to fund such programs with large grants to establish libraries and multi-year acquisition programs.

Two problems are finding adequately trained, politically reliable staff and finding the right mechanism to create programs at state-run universities where anti-Americanism runs high. At the beginning, it may be useful for the government to encourage a consortium of U.S. universities to work together to establish a network of distance-education programs (i.e., via internet) associated with local universities. Over time, full-scale programs could be established by leveraging public funds with private foundation grants.

Perhaps the most important aspect will be finding a mechanism to entice students who may be skeptical about job prospects—after all, what does one do in Cairo, Casablanca, or Muscat with a degree in American studies? Here, the U.S. government should work hand-in-hand with local American chambers of commerce and local branches of U.S. nongovernment institutions throughout the Middle East to establish mentoring and internship programs with a goal of guaranteeing a job to every graduate of an American studies program.

An especially high priority should be placed on investing in expanded English-language training programs throughout the region. English is the gateway into American culture and the global community, and expanding access to it for Middle Easterners provides the best chance for the success of all other public diplomacy efforts. Given that the content of much English teaching material focuses on sympathetic themes like democracy, free markets, and American studies, this provides double bang for the buck—not only do students equip themselves with an essential language tool to compete in the global economy, but they familiarize themselves with U.S. culture, politics, and society in the process. Additional funding for "teaching the teachers" programs will be money well spent.

(One specialized area where a U.S. initiative—working in tandem with U.S. and local Arab educators—can make headway is in Holocaust education for Arab students. A survey of Holocaust and tolerance-related institutions here and abroad reveals that not a single module, text, or program for Holocaust education exists in an Arab country, even within the context of studying twentieth-century history, "genocides" around the world, or tolerance education—perhaps one reason why there is so much misinformation, let alone denial, on the subject throughout the Middle East.)

At the same time, the U.S. government should do more to attract students to colleges and universities inside the United States, direct them to appropriate programs, and provide guidance, counseling, and, one should note, thorough oversight throughout their stay (and until their departure). This would require developing educational advising networks at U.S. embassies throughout the region, raising the level of expertise of overseas advisors, establishing full-time postings for regional educational coordinators, and equipping posts with up-to-date technology. And once in the United States, Middle Eastern students comprise an excellent target audience for special public diplomacy outreach programs, such as regular lectures by U.S. officials at universities with large Middle Eastern student populations.

Exchanges

Regrettably, one of the lessons of September 11, evidenced by the months and years spent in America by the perpetrators, is that familiarity does not always breed sympathy, let alone friendship. Nevertheless, exchange programs have, over time, proven to be useful and relatively cost-effective tools in building positive relationships, one person at a time. Indeed, that is the secret of their success—they need to be well targeted, individually designed, long enough to make a lasting impression, but not too long.

One fine program that deserves expansion is the Humphrey Fellowships, which bring mid-career professionals to the United States. With extra funding, overseas posts can identify a wider range of prospects, especially in the fields of NGO development, public health, journalism, education, and the environment. Here, it is important to seek out future and potential leaders to bring to America and not use fellowships to award personal friendships already made or to provide payback to political cronies of local officials. U.S. diplomats abroad need to be especially creative about recruiting such fellows, using the program both to encourage incipient signs of pro-Americanism and as a corrective measure for people whose critical views are not well-entrenched. Reaching out to less traditional applicants beyond the upper-crust elite would be beneficial, not least to encourage an appreciation for meritocracy as a core American value.

International visitor programs are also useful and constructive, but they too need to be more targeted than has been the case in recent years. Due to budget cuts, visitors have been lumped together into large and often unwieldy groups, sometimes with participants from a dozen or more countries. The result has been that visitors often learn much about other cultures and countries from their fellow visitors but less about U.S. society. In general, it is better to provide specialized (and more expensive) programming to a smaller group for a shorter time than a less carefully designed program to a larger group for a larger period of time. Targeted groups should include journalists, educators, legislators, judges, and community leaders. A special focus—here and throughout the public diplomacy campaign—needs to be made on women and youth.

Sending Americans abroad to act as goodwill ambassadors can be beneficial, too, though the political sensitivities are higher than hosting foreign visitors (i.e., every American sent abroad is assumed to represent the U.S. government) and a series of one-off contacts with a visiting American is less likely to leave a lasting impression than an immersion visit by a Middle Easterner to the United States. Sending Americans as goodwill ambassadors abroad requires especially close vetting. There are three categories of such private individuals: practical ambassadors (e.g., town managers, civic leaders, local health and education officials), cultural ambassadors (e.g., musicians, artists), and educational ambassadors (e.g., professors speaking on U.S. Middle East policy, American Muslims lecturing on religious tolerance in the United States). The first group should be most highly prized and preferred. In general, the first and second together are far more important—and pose much less risk of funding the wrong type of spokesperson—than the third. Also, to take full advantage of such visits, it is important that special consideration be given to facilitating ongoing, follow-up relations between visitors and local contacts, creating long-term, multi-year theme programs rather than a series of disparate speakers and topics, and studying ways to deepen the value of such exchanges.

Conclusion

In a public diplomacy campaign, like the war against terror itself, there will be no quick victories and few demonstrable successes. In devising this campaign, it is better to get it right than to do it fast; better to make incremental progress than risk damage through grandiose schemes gone awry; and better to draw on the expertise of those who have been successful in other parts of the globe at other periods of time rather than leave the project to regionalists who may be more committed to understanding local cultures than projecting our own. Even with maximum funding, the cumulative impact of all the initiatives described above will only be felt over time and, regrettably, on the margin. But it is important that the United States make the effort to provide Middle Easterners with the opportunity to know about our politics, government, policies, and way of life and, on that basis, to make informed choices about their support for or opposition to the United States and how they wish to build their own future and own societies.

PART II

What We Do Wrong

Battling for Hearts and Minds
in the Middle East

September 2002

I N TERMS OF PUBLIC DIPLOMACY, THE U.S. GOVERNMENT'S
record since September 11 is poor. This failing grade is due to a com-
bination of factors: faulty strategic direction from public diplomacy
policymakers, who have put a premium on a well-intentioned but highly
counterproductive effort "to be liked" at the expense of policy advocacy;
flawed tactical decisions that have lent an aura of endorsement to some of
the most virulent critics (and critiques) of U.S. interests and policy; a lack of
speed and creativity in taking advantage of the post–September 11 window to
develop and implement new public diplomacy projects and initiatives (some
of which are actually resurrected old projects that were prematurely termi-
nated); and over-reliance on the powers of broadcasting and a concomitant
lack of attention and adequate funding to medium- and long-term aspects
of the "hearts and minds" campaign. An assessment of the past year suggests
that the heart of the problem lies in Washington, not in the field, where most
public diplomacy professionals toil with woefully inadequate resources and
poor policy direction. Even in the field, however, some are reluctant to press
the case for U.S. policy, preferring instead to focus efforts on winning admiration for and sympathy with U.S. values.

Key Problems

- **"We don't have a correct definition of who the good guys are and who
  the bad guys are."** Condemnation of the September 11 attacks should

Originally published as *PolicyWatch* number 657, September 17, 2002.

not be the sole criterion for determining America's allies in the war on terror; too many theologians, scholars, and leaders in Arab and Muslim countries condemn al-Qaeda while glorifying the suicide terrorists of Hamas and Islamic Jihad and/or fueling the virulent anti-Americanism in regional media. Touting the September 11 condemnations by such clerics as the Qatari Yusuf al-Qaradawi (who endorsed suicide bombings) and Saudi Shaykh Abdul Rahman al-Sudais (who described Jews as "scum of humanity . . . the rats of the world . . . pigs and monkeys") in the State Department's flagship "Network of Terrorism" booklet is a mistake, as is any effort by senior officials to "dialogue" with such terrorist fellow-travelers as the Islamic Action Front in Jordan. These efforts only provide succor to America's enemies and undermine its true friends.

- **"We lend support to the wrong people in the culture wars being fought in Arab and Muslim societies."** In the war on terror, America's allies (current and future) are the liberalizing, modernizing forces fighting against the cultural totalitarianism gaining ground throughout the Middle East. Yet, the State Department's flagship outreach website—"Muslim Life in America"—sends precisely the wrong message to such forces. (This subsite is featured on the website of every U.S. embassy in the Middle East and is found on the State Department's International Information Programs website, which reportedly receives 60 million hits per year.) For example, in its goodhearted but profoundly counterproductive effort to project American tolerance abroad, this website projects the image that virtually all American Muslim women (and the large majority of American Muslim girls) are veiled, hardly a message of support to the Afghan women now free to choose whether to wear the burqa; to Iranian women fighting to throw off the chador; or to Turkish women, whose contribution to building a democracy in an overwhelmingly Muslim state should be celebrated. The same U.S. government website offers a ludicrous dictionary of Islamic terminology (e.g., the definition of "jihad" says that the term "should not be confused with Holy War, which does not exist in Islam") and highlights quotations by U.S. experts who otherwise hold views diametrically opposed to U.S. policy (e.g., a news story that features a University of Michigan professor who has written a Middle East politics curriculum for high school teachers that counsels "minimal reference to terrorism" because, as he states, "[E]ven people who have engaged in attacks on innocent civilians have legitimate human interests in security, dignity, and self-government").

- **"We place too much emphasis on advertising America's religious tolerance and not enough on advocating policy."** A review of the "Fact Sheet for Public Diplomacy in Action" in the State Department's "Press Kit for the War on Terror" underscores the fact that the lion's share of the department's public diplomacy efforts are aimed at promoting America's record of religious tolerance to Muslim and Arab states and peoples. (Incidentally, the fact sheet includes not a word about public diplomacy efforts since September 11 to Europe, Latin America, China, India, or other predominantly non-Muslim parts of the world.) Such a strategy makes little sense in light of the fact that America's record on tolerance is not a central issue for the vast majority of Middle Easterners. Indeed, if anything, most would say that Americans are too tolerant—too promiscuous, too libertine, too open to various lifestyles and competing views of the world. In other words, the U.S. government is spending much of its time fighting the wrong war.

Defining Appropriate Goals for Public Diplomacy

For the Middle East, the "right" public diplomacy war should be defined modestly as the campaign to ensure that the United States—its leaders, spokesmen, and citizens—get a fair hearing, not a hearing dominated by the xenophobic, anti-Western, anti-American, anti-Semitic media and old-style educational systems that tend to dominate in many countries. Regrettably, even this modest goal does not seem to be shared by the policymakers who shape the U.S. public diplomacy effort.

In her June 11, 2002, congressional testimony, Undersecretary of State for Public Diplomacy Charlotte Beers outlined three strategic goals for U.S. public diplomacy abroad: representing American values and beliefs; demonstrating the opportunities that result from democratization, good governance, and open markets; and supporting the education of the young. Although all of these goals are necessary, this "mission statement" is sorely insufficient.

First, it does not include any aspect of policy advocacy. (As defined once by the U.S. Advisory Commission on Public Diplomacy, "public diplomacy" is "the communication of U.S. interests and ideals beyond governments to foreign publics.") Although public diplomacy encompasses more than policy advocacy, such advocacy must be at the core of all public diplomacy campaigns. It is essential to have spokespeople for the United States advocating U.S. policy, not just celebrating American values.

Second, it is insufficient to argue that the United States merely "supports education of the young." Washington needs to be concerned with the content of education, not just the fact of education; the United States should focus on what Middle Easterners are learning, reading, hearing, and watching. This has four components:

1. The United States should aggressively and consistently (yet always deliberately and factually) combat virulent anti-American propaganda that passes for journalism in many countries. Remarkably, there appears to be no single office or contact at the State Department with specific responsibility for this task.

2. The United States should be competing for the minds of young Muslims through education. There are many ways to do this: sending books overseas; training teachers; participating in curriculum reform; matching American and Middle Eastern universities and technical-training institutes; fostering more American studies programs; and so forth. A good place to start is distance learning, which costs little and is relatively easy to manage. Regrettably, there is not a single Middle East-related project referenced on the website of the federal government's Interagency Working Group on this issue.

3. The United States should be judicious in expanding its broadcasting efforts in the Middle East. The new Radio Sawa is an innovative approach to gaining market share and should be supported, so long as the early emphasis on music begins to give way to substantive content. At the same time, the Bush administration should be wary of plans to duplicate Sawa's model elsewhere in the region; for example, Voice of America-Persian has a much greater and more loyal following than Voice of America-Arabic ever did, and it should not simply be jettisoned in favor of a Persian variant of Sawa. More important, Washington should be wary of trying to apply the Sawa model to satellite television. Not only have U.S. government broadcasters not yet fully grappled with the difficulties of juggling between surrogate and nonsurrogate objectives, but at the moment there is no conceivable, acceptable programming that could compete with the sensationalism of existing Arab satellite television channels. For the foreseeable future, the money targeted for a U.S. government experiment in satellite television would be better spent on other projects.

4. Perhaps most important, the Bush administration should consider a substantial increase in funding for English-language training abroad, which may be the most valuable marginal dollar that could be spent for public diplomacy. With a working knowledge of English, young Arabs and Muslims around the world can access existing U.S. satellite television, U.S. newspapers and magazines, and U.S. educational opportunities, listening to U.S. leaders and ordinary Americans without the filter of translation. Through English, young people enter a portal to globalization that, almost by definition, gives America a chance to be heard. According to the State Department's Bureau of Educational and Cultural Affairs, the U.S. government spent a paltry $10 million worldwide in support of English-language teaching in 2001, with only about $1 million targeted at the Middle East. The price of existing U.S.-sponsored English-language training programs is often prohibitive, amounting (in some places) to a half or more of a country's per capita income. Instead of pricing English out of the market for the vast majority of Middle Easterners, the United States should make English education affordable to all. Washington should set a goal of becoming as efficient in exporting English as Wahhabis are in exporting their brand of Islam to madrasas around the world.

Conclusion

Over the past year, the Bush administration has done much right in the war on terrorism. Sadly, its public diplomacy effort is not one of those successes. Washington does have some positive accomplishments to its credit. For example, there are some excellent pro-democracy websites produced by the State Department that appear on some (though not all) Middle East embassy websites, and some embassies have undertaken innovative programming of their own with local media and schools. In general, however, U.S. public diplomacy over the past year has emphasized the wrong priorities, the wrong message, and the wrong programs. Thankfully, battling for hearts and minds is a long-term project, and it is not too late for the United States to fight the good fight. But Washington does have a lot of catching up to do.

We're Losing the Battle for Hearts and Minds

September 2002

W ITH HIGH-PROFILE ARRESTS FROM UPSTATE NEW YORK
to faraway Karachi, recent days have been good for the good guys
in the "war on terrorism." But in one critical arena—the battle
for hearts and minds in the Middle East, known in Beltway-speak as "public
diplomacy"—the United States isn't even putting up a fight.

Public diplomacy is, according to one official U.S. government definition,
"the communication of U.S. interests and ideals to foreign publics." At its
core, public diplomacy is about ensuring that our policies get a fair hearing
in the court of international public opinion.

Regrettably, the year since the September 11 attacks has seen the State
Department devise a feel-good public diplomacy campaign that is more
about being liked than being understood.

Our natural allies in the war on terror are beleaguered moderates throughout the Middle East fighting against cultural totalitarianism. But U.S. officials have produced publications, websites, and programs that undermine
our friends and lend endorsement to our adversaries.

A prime example is the State Department's premier outreach website, "Muslim Life in America," (http://usinfo.state.gov/products/pubs/muslimlife/)
which is featured on the home page of every U.S. embassy in the Middle
East. In its effort to project the image of a tolerant America to Muslims
around the world, this site includes a collage of about fifty photos in which
virtually every adult woman and most girls are veiled or wearing head scarves.
Not only does that misrepresent American Muslim women but it also sends
precisely the wrong message to Afghan women now free to choose whether

Originally published in the *Los Angeles Times*, September 20, 2002.

to wear the burqa, to Iranian women fighting to throw off the chador and to Turkish women at the vanguard of building democracy in an overwhelmingly Muslim state.

Another government website (http://usinfo.state.gov/usa/islam/overview. htm) offers a ludicrous dictionary of Islamic terminology that states, for example, that "jihad should not be confused with Holy War, [which] does not exist in Islam"—a position held by no serious scholar of Islam.

The problem goes beyond websites. Government publications, such as the widely disseminated booklet "Network of Terrorism," show that we foolishly seek common cause with many in the Middle East by celebrating the fair-weather condemnations of the September 11 attacks by prominent Muslim clerics who otherwise revel in the killings of innocents (in Israel) through suicide bombings.

Taken in small doses, an effort to identify common values among different cultures and to emphasize abroad the exemplary record of U.S. religious tolerance makes sense. But to make this campaign the centerpiece of our public diplomacy, especially at the exclusion of policy advocacy, is to fight the wrong war. That is one of the key findings of a just-published report of the U.S. Advisory Commission on Public Diplomacy. For most Middle Easterners, the U.S. record on tolerance is not a central issue. Indeed, if anything, most would say we are too tolerant—too promiscuous, too libertine, too open to various lifestyles.

The crux of the problem is that Washington has sent the message to our diplomats abroad to win admiration for our values at the expense of the admittedly uncomfortable task of advocating our policies. Indeed, when our most senior public diplomacy official—Undersecretary of State Charlotte Beers, a former advertising executive—outlined her strategic goals before Congress in June 2002, advocating U.S. interests and policies didn't even make the list.

To fight the right war, we need to fight the xenophobic, anti-Western, anti-American media and old-style educational systems that dominate throughout the Middle East, reach out to help our hardy but lonely allies and do more to provide Arabs and Muslims with the tools, such as English language training, to access American politics, culture and society for themselves.

On September 12, 2002, President Bush delivered an outstanding address at the United Nations that advocated our policies on Iraq and promoted our values of fair play, self-reliance and prudent multilateralism. With proper direction, our diplomats too can project both our policies and our values. As it is, our public diplomacy is doing as much harm as good.

Voices Who Speak For
(and Against) Us

December 2002

FROM INDONESIA TO PAKISTAN, MUSLIMS TUNING INTO television after breaking Ramadan fasts this month are viewing a smorgasbord of U.S.-funded advertisements praising religious tolerance in America. Designed to highlight an appealing attribute of U.S. society, these thirty-second spots seem harmless, though most likely ineffectual in countering anti-Americanism. On closer inspection, however, this $15 million ad campaign is just the most high-profile example of a policy of "dumbing down" our outreach to Muslim peoples.

Since September 11, the Bush administration has been fighting two wars. One, against terror, has been fought with creativity and vigor; another, for the hearts and minds of the world's Muslims, has been waged with a baffling lack of clarity and confidence. Instead of recognizing that millions of Muslims dislike America because of the alleged injustice of our policies on contentious issues such as terrorism, Iraq, and Israel, we have chosen to believe that if only Muslims knew us better—our society, values, and culture—they would hate us less. Hence, the administration's "public diplomacy"—outreach to people in foreign countries over the heads of foreign governments—focuses disproportionately on "soft" topics, such as values, while shying away from advocating the foreign policies many Muslims don't like and may, in fact, not know enough about.

A prime example is the State Department's "speakers program," which sends U.S. specialists abroad or arranges for them to speak to foreign audiences via digital video conference. In the public diplomacy arsenal, the "speakers program" has special attraction. Dispatching one person abroad is

Originally published in the *Washington Post*, December 1, 2002.

easy to organize and offers a quick response to changing national priorities. Once in the field, speakers can leave a powerful personal imprint on the message they are transmitting.

In the year after September 11, 2001, about 1,600 such programs were planned or implemented, reaching tens of thousands of nongovernmental elites, such as journalists, scholars and businesspeople. Many of these programs offered valuable information on such items as new ways to fight corruption or battle drug abuse. Other speakers opened vistas of Americana—such as black history or American poetry—in corners of the world that have little contact with our culture.

While important, these issues hardly reflect the core mission of public diplomacy, which is to inform people overseas about U.S. policy. In fact, a review of data prepared by the State Department's Office of International Information Programs shows how reluctant Foggy Bottom is to dispatch speakers to address contentious national security issues rather than soft topics such as religious tolerance.

According to State's own accounting, twice as much money was spent on speakers programs about "American Life and Values" than about the themes of "combating terrorism," "Middle East peace," "weapons of mass destruction," and "Iraq"—combined. In a year that saw war against al-Qaeda and the Taliban, the total spent on speakers sent abroad to talk about Afghanistan was zero.

The post–September 11 agenda is mostly avoided by these speakers, especially those who visit the Muslim world. Of the approximately 125 programs convened in Muslim-majority countries in the Middle East or Asia, fewer than twenty touched on any policy issue. Amazingly, "terrorism" was the stated theme of just five. More than four times as many programs (twenty-two) focused on the role of Arabs or Muslims in American society. State sent out a more balanced group to non-Muslim-majority countries, where twice as many speakers discussed terrorism as those who discussed issues of domestic tolerance in America. Nine officers from the New York City Police and Fire departments were dispatched abroad to talk about their moving September 11 experiences, but none was sent to a Muslim nation.

If, at a time of war, that mix seems skewed, then so, too, does the composition of the group of "experts" speaking on America's behalf. More than 40 percent of programs on Islam, Arabs and Muslims in America, or on religious tolerance within the United States, featured current or former representatives of domestic Arab or Muslim advocacy organizations. Many of the speakers, such as the American Muslim Council's former executive director Aly Abuzaakouk (who was sent to Nigeria) and communications director Faiz Rahman (who spoke via teleconference to Bulgaria), have either publicly minimized the threat posed by bin Ladenism or criticized the Bush administration's anti-terror or Middle East policies. Advocates of these positions—while legitimate in a domestic political debate—are hardly the sort of messengers the administration should want to promote in its diplomacy abroad.

Similarly, many of the scholars recruited to talk about Islam in America have soft-pedaled the threat from radical Islamists for years. Especially prominent is the group from Georgetown University, which alone provided 40 percent of the Islam-related speakers. Here, the list includes John Esposito, founder of Georgetown's Center for Muslim-Christian Understanding, whose best-selling 1992 book *The Islamic Threat: Myth or Reality* was dedicated to the proposition that Islamist threats to our national security would be increasingly unlikely. Five other current or former associates of the center were also State Department speakers.

The inclusion of some of the academics on an official government speakers list is truly stunning. A prime example is Asma Barlas, political science professor at Ithaca College, who spoke via teleconference to Indian elites on "Women and Islam." Apparently, no one at State checked her website, a collection of blame-America-first tirades, such as, "When we ask, 'Why do they hate us?' I believe it is because we don't want to ask the question we should be asking: Why do we hate and oppress them?" (*Ithaca College Quarterly*, 2001), or "[I]t is difficult to regard this as a war rather than as terrorism" (*Daily Times*, Pakistan, June 18, 2002).

All told, the makeup of the Islam-related speakers list provides a self-defeating twist on the legislation governing "public diplomacy," the Smith-Mundt Act of 1948. That law authorized the federal government "to disseminate abroad information about the United States, its people, and its policies." Nowhere does the law suggest that advertising our diversity needs to clash with the advocating of our policies.

To be sure, finding the right mix of people to speak on behalf of America overseas is not easy. Speakers should be independent, not government surrogates, and constructive critiques of U.S. policy should be tolerated. But we should not enlist speakers whose views lend succor to our enemies.

State sometimes got it right. The choice of speakers dispatched to Europe and Latin America, replete with national security experts from both Democratic and Republican administrations, shows a healthy respect for the need to explain America's case, leavened with a sense of the honest debate taking place at home.

In addressing Muslim issues or Muslim countries, however, we have our priorities backward. With a few noteworthy exceptions, such as the courageous Iranian feminist Azar Nafisi, now at Johns Hopkins University, we, too, often have exported our loudest critics, with an official stamp of approval, rather than dispatching experts who could present—heaven forbid!—robust expositions of our policies.

Privately, well-meaning State Department officials recognize that the speakers program needs fixing and say they are righting the course. But the two themes chosen for special attention in the coming year—"Outreach to the Muslim World" and "Perceptions of U.S. Unilateralism"—echo the self-defeating programming of the past. We need to explain our perceptions of ourselves and the world, not our views of their views of our views.

Like other skewed aspects of the administration's public diplomacy—such as official publications that highlight condemnations of the September 11 attacks by Muslim clerics famous for their praise of other suicide bombings—fixing our public diplomacy requires a wholesale change of approach. Washington's public-diplomacy designers need to operate on the basis that America is, in fact, at war. Advertising our diversity may be a worthy goal in times of peace, but we don't have that luxury today. At a time when the world looks to us for clarity of purpose, activist naysayers should not be chosen to speak abroad under the State Department banner.

Moreover, we need to take Muslim elites seriously. Values are important— they are what America is all about. But there is scant evidence that Muslim crowds from Cairo to Karachi burn Uncle Sam in effigy because of perceptions about intolerance toward their co-religionists in America. Many may never support our policies on terrorism, Iraq, and Israel, but the key elites in Muslim-majority countries are sophisticated people who deserve frank talk. Rather than shy away from our policies, we should defend them. Serving up a diet of fluff is not just wrong, it's condescending, a foreign policy version of what President Bush, in another context, called the "subtle bigotry of low expectations."

The battle for hearts and minds begins with respect. Our current public diplomacy respects neither the citizenry it claims to represent nor the Arabs and Muslims it is designed to impress; as such, it is doomed to fail. If we change that dynamic, we at least stand a chance of winning this fight.

Wrong Answer to al-Jazeera

April 2003

TO COMBAT WHAT IS WIDELY VIEWED AS THE SLANTED
news coverage of Arab satellite stations, the White House and Congress are joining forces to spend tens—perhaps hundreds—of millions
of dollars to launch an official Arabic-language U.S. government competitor.
Unfortunately, it has a chance of turning out to be one of this country's most
ill-conceived and wasteful experiments ever in public diplomacy.

At first blush the argument in support of what is called the "Middle East
Television Network"—METN—is compelling. Most Arabs watch television
as their principal source of news and find satellite stations more credible and
interesting than their local, state-controlled networks. Most satellite stations,
including the widely known al-Jazeera, present the news through an anti-
American lens; none projects a dispassionate, analytical approach to news, let
alone a pro-American tilt. The United States has been surrendering the field
to its enemies, it is argued.

Advocates then cite the "success story" of recent U.S. government radio
initiatives in the Middle East. Topping the list is the new Radio Sawa, a 24-7
operation that has four regional streams, all built around an innovative mix of
Western and Arabic popular music. Preliminary listener numbers show that
Sawa appears to have attracted a significant following. The patrons of satellite television—the Broadcasting Board of Governors, a semi-independent
body that oversees all U.S. government international broadcasting—promise
a similar success story on a much larger scale.

So far the idea has elicited cheers from the Bush administration as well
as Capitol Hill. The result was a $30 million request for METN in Presi-

---

Originally published in the *Washington Post*, April 4, 2003.

dent Bush's 2004 budget and more in the wartime supplemental. Not to be outdone, the House and the Senate, in their versions of pending legislation, propose even more.

The only problem is that no one seems to have asked three critical questions: What precisely is the market niche for this station? What will its programmatic content be? And is this the most effective and efficient way to spend a new, large pot of public diplomacy money?

METN will fail for the same reason that Radio Sawa appears to have succeeded. Whereas the Middle East radio market is tightly controlled by local regimes, with very few transnational options available (such as the BBC or Radio Monte Carlo), the regional television market is overflowing with choice. Basic satellite service in a country such as Morocco, for example, without any paid or pirated supplement, provides access to five satellites with dozens of Arabic-language stations. At any moment of the day, one can watch news shows, documentaries, sitcoms, soap operas, MTV imitators or dubbed Hollywood movies. Precisely which niche is METN supposed to fill?

As for content, the problem is that no conceivable programming for METN news shows would meet the dual test of popularity abroad and political correctness at home. Al-Jazeera and other Arabic satellite news channels won popularity because of their lurid sensationalism and no-holds-barred debates. Viewers tune in to see graphic details of the bloody side of Israeli retaliation to Palestinian terrorism and talk shows that feature the most outlandish radicals, such as spokesmen for the Taliban, Hizballah, or Saddam Hussein, duking it out with establishment mandarins.

Surely METN cannot try to be more sensationalist than al-Jazeera. Few in Congress are going to like subsidizing TV time for Iranian mullahs or the proud parents of Palestinian suicide bombers. The alternative would be PBS-style highbrow, high-quality news shows. That sounds great, but the reality is that such shows are likely to gain even fewer viewers in the saturated Middle East satellite market than PBS does in the U.S. market.

The upscale, well-educated Arab PBS market is hardly worth a nine-digit investment when the supposed target is angry, unemployed twentysome-things. Indeed, if the goal is to ensure satellite access for Middle Easterners to professional news that gives America a fair hearing, it would be much cheaper to offer tax incentives to U.S. broadcasters to perform the public service of dubbing and then duplicating their news in Arabic. The fact that CNN, CNBC and Fox are nongovernmental enterprises ensures far greater credibility than what is possible for METN. This more credible, less expensive plan would free millions of dollars for underfunded public diplomacy projects of proven value.

Before taxpayers are asked to buy into METN, due diligence is in order. So far, it hasn't happened.

PART III

What We Do Right

Still Open to Arabs

November 2003

HAVE ONEROUS POST–SEPTEMBER 11 VISA REQUIREMENTS denied young Arabs access to American colleges and universities? That charge was made by the authors of the "Arab Human Development Report," published last month and prepared by respected Arab researchers under the auspices of the U.N. Development Program. Their condemnation of Washington's alleged anti-Arab bias, post–September 11, received headline coverage in national newspapers.

Specifically, the report accused the Bush administration of "extreme" counterterrorism policies that "led to the erosion of civil and political liberties . . . diminishing the welfare of Arabs and Muslims living, studying or traveling abroad." The result, it argues, was the "cutting off [of] knowledge acquisition opportunities for young Arabs." The effect of these policies, the report claimed, was "an average 30 percent drop in Arab student enrollment in U.S. colleges and universities between 1999 and 2002."

If true, that accusation would be a black stain on America's traditional openness to foreign students, and it would undermine the Bush administration's strategy of combating bin Ladenism by opening young Arab hearts and minds to one of America's showcase exports: its institutions of higher education.

But the charge is not true.

The small print in the report shows that the claim of a "30 percent drop" is derived from student enrollment numbers kept by just four Arab missions to the United Nations—Saudi Arabia, Qatar, Oman and Yemen. Why the fine Arab scholars who contributed to the report would rely on data on just

Originally published in the *Baltimore Sun*, November 28, 2003.

four of twenty-two Arab countries, drawn from such an odd source, is bewildering. Even so, the raw numbers provided by these missions tell a somewhat different story.

According to the Arab missions, Saudi Arabia—which whisked hundreds of nationals out of the United States in the immediate aftermath of September 11, well before the passage of the USA Patriot Act—does indeed show a 31 percent drop in enrollment. But because of the disproportionately large number of Saudi students in the United States, the Saudi share of the enrollment decrease was 88 percent of the total decrease.

In essence, the hasty Saudi pilgrimage home skewed the overall story. By contrast, for example, students from Yemen—itself a source of considerable anti-U.S. terrorism, such as the bombing of the USS Cole—showed barely any enrollment drop (188 students in 1999, 181 students in 2002).

A more comprehensive and nuanced view of the issue can be found in the statistics compiled by the Institute of International Education. The IIE's annual Open Doors survey provides a detailed breakdown of foreign students in the United States that goes back more than a decade.

The big story there is the roller-coaster fluctuation in Arab enrollment at U.S. universities. Enrollment from many Arab countries has been dropping for years. Yemen, for example, had 50 percent more students in the United States in 1992 than in 1999; Qatar's numbers dropped steadily every year between 1992 and 1997, only picking up in 1998. All of North Africa declined in the first half of the 1990s and increased in the second half.

Chief among the many reasons for this was the Arab economic recession of the post-oil-glut years, which even compelled oil exporters to tighten their belts on subsidizing overseas education. Indeed, the Arab scholars' report does not even mention that many Persian Gulf states long ago began instituting measures to limit the numbers of students going abroad, opting instead to expand less costly opportunities at home.

But didn't America's post–September 11 anti-terrorism policies, especially stiffer visa rules, still drive tens of thousands of Arab students away from our universities? It is undoubtedly true that many students suffered inconvenience and some may have, as a result, chosen to study elsewhere; getting the kinks out of the new visa system is an important priority. But the charge itself is simply false.

This month, the IIE issued a report showing just a 10 percent decrease in Middle East student enrollment in 2002-2003, the first full academic year since September 11. While Saudis did register a steep decline, the overall statistics mean that most Arab countries are continuing to send substantial numbers of students to U.S. schools.

Indeed, there is no support for the accusation of a "30 percent drop" from pre–September 11 levels. According to the IIE, there were actually 6 percent more students from all Middle East countries enrolled in U.S. universities in 2002-2003 than in 1998-1999. ("Middle East" includes some non-Arab countries, such as Iran and Turkey, but all are governed by the new visa regulations.)

While the anecdotal evidence gets the headlines, the statistics tell the story: despite September 11, the doors to American higher education remain open to Arab students.

Winning Over Arabs,
One Dancer at a Time

March 2004

NOW FOR SOMETHING COMPLETELY DIFFERENT . . . A good news story about U.S. outreach toward Arabs. On Tuesday, March 16, 2004, the Pew Foundation released shocking new poll numbers about the country where my family and I have been living for the past two years—the Kingdom of Morocco. According to the Pew findings, 45 percent of Moroccans have a favorable view of Osama bin Laden and 66 percent consider suicide bombings against American and other Western interests justifiable. The fact that so many of those implicated in the Madrid train bombings were reportedly of Moroccan origin—as has been the case with most al-Qaeda cells unearthed in Europe—lends real-life urgency to these statistics.

Public diplomacy—the art of reaching over the heads of governments and speaking directly to their people—is that aspect of U.S. foreign policy tasked with chipping away at this mountain of mistrust. Living in Rabat, the capital of this country of thirty million, I have had the opportunity of seeing U.S. public diplomacy in action. Frankly, it is not always a pretty sight.

But if March 16 brought bad news, it also was the day I witnessed American public diplomacy at its finest.

The setting was the Muhammad V Auditorium, the local Carnegie Hall. Rabat is not exactly a happening place, so when the American embassy advertised a free performance of the New York–based Battery Park Dance Company, hundreds flocked to see it.

The program got off to a good start with an understated yet effective welcoming address by the U.S. embassy's cultural affairs officer. His remarks

Previously unpublished essay.

included a moment of silence for the victims of two recent disasters that have, for different reasons, shaken local society: the recent earthquake along Morocco's Mediterranean coast and the previous week's terrorist attack in Madrid. Then, he closed with the tantalizing promise of a postperformance surprise. The fact that the diplomat spoke in well-crafted if American-accented French should not be taken for granted. At a previous embassy musical event, the hostess welcomed the French- and Arabic-speaking crowd in well-crafted if American-accented English. I understood what she was saying but I was in a distinct minority.

For the next ninety minutes, the audience was entertained by a thoroughly professional performance of modern dance (at least it certainly seemed to be thoroughly professional to me, someone who knows nothing about modern dance). But the electric moment—the great success for America—is what came after the curtain call.

Evidently, members of the Battery Park troupe had spent several days with inner-city kids in Rabat and Casablanca, holding dance tutorials. When the formal show concluded, the director, Jonathan Hollander, came on stage and unveiled the surprise—a group of about twenty Moroccan youngsters, mostly teenagers, who had been practicing with the pros. Dressed in baggy pants, bandanas, and name-brand sneakers, these kids could have been from Anywhere, USA.

One of the Americans then led two Moroccans—a young man named Moulay and a young woman named Simone—through a series of fast-paced dance moves. Seeing their compatriots performing on stage, the audience cheered.

Then came the showstopper: a half-dozen young Moroccan men thrilling the audience with the sort of break dancing that makes tongues wag, eyes bulge, and hands clap. At first, one of the American dancers led them, keeping an eye on the dance line, ensuring his charges kept pace with the rhythm of the music, but before long he moved off. The Moroccans had center stage.

The crowd went wild, marveling at the acrobatics, the athleticism, the power of these young dancers, *their* young dancers. They brought the house down.

America hasn't had as good a night here in a long time. Sure, we register strategic successes, such as the recently inked U.S.-Morocco Free Trade Agreement, only the second with an Arab country. But we don't so easily win friends like those kids on stage, who are precisely the type to fit the profile of "angry young men," the sort who strap dynamite around their waists—or, in Spain's case, plant cell-phone bombs—that kill hundreds of innocents.

But thanks to the power of art, dance, and music, the young Moroccans connected to America and to the Americans who helped bring alive their natural talent. And the hundreds of people in the audience—admittedly, hundreds of upper-class Moroccans, ministers, diplomats, entrepreneurs, the sort who would spend an evening devoted to modern dance—connected too. Perhaps their most important connection was to the dancers themselves, those very same "angry young men" usually viewed in elite circles as a "problem" or a "burden," people to be "handled" or "managed," but rarely as people brimming with promise. In the battle against extremism and radicalism, making this kind of connection among Arabs is no less important than making the connection between Arabs and Americans.

I am not so naïve as to think that one, or even one hundred, dance troupes are going to remedy whatever ailment leads two-thirds of Moroccans to tell pollsters they find nothing objectionable about suicide bombings. But I do know that no Moroccan left the Muhammad V Auditorium on Tuesday evening, March 16, with the same attitude as when he or she entered about art, the United States, and the God-given talents of young Moroccan men and women. That's progress. And when the clouds are as dark as they often seem to be, even the narrowest of silver linings will do.

American Schools Abroad
Have a Big Part to Play

December 2003

L IKE LEGIONS OF OTHER PROUD PARENTS, MY WIFE AND I
sat beaming in the audience earlier this month, video camera in hand,
as our son Benji, six, stood with his fellow first-graders on the stage
of his school auditorium and sang a medley of holiday songs. The adorably
cute, multicultural program included Christmas favorites, a few Hanukkah
melodies and even tunes in Swedish, Japanese and Arabic.

What made our son's concert special is that he is a student at the Rabat
American School, in the capital of Morocco, a country of thirty million
Muslims, a population rattled by a wave of suicide bombings just six months
ago. In this context, Benji's elementary school winter concert was an event of
prime importance to U.S. national security.

Ever since September 11, experts have debated how to win the battle for
hearts and minds among the world's 300 million Arabs and 1.2 billion Muslims. Everyone seems to have the magic bullet—from creating Arabic language satellite television stations that counter sensationalist local media to
building American style universities overseas so local students don't have to
run the visa gauntlet to come to the United States. Many of these ideas have
multimillion dollar pricetags.

When I saw young Ahmed introduce a chorus of "Dreidel, Dreidel," I real-
ized that American schools, 185 spread over 132 countries, are already playing
a vital role in the international culture wars and deserve more support.

Most American schools are nonprofit, nondenominational, coeducation
institutions founded by overseas communities of American citizens and usually owned and operated by local parents associations. They are designed to

Originally published in the *International Herald Tribune*, December 23, 2003.

provide a fully accredited, English-language, U.S.-style curriculum, leavened with study of local languages, to prepare students to enter higher education in the United States.

What makes American schools a strategic asset is the fact that non-Americans flock to them. Of the nearly 100,000 students enrolled in such schools around the world, more than 70 percent are not American, fairly evenly divided between local and third-country students. My son's class of twenty-one kids, for example, has a half-dozen Moroccans plus students from Algeria, Brunei, Italy, Sweden, Britain, Germany, Japan, and South Korea—with just four Americans.

Students at these schools learn how to ask questions, be curious, solve problems and accept differences. They study Thanksgiving, George Washington, and Martin Luther King while finding a way to celebrate the various nationalities each brings to the classroom. Every student leaves with a facility in English and an appreciation for critical thinking and cultural diversity that represent American education at its best. While these schools may only benefit relatively few children, their impact is profound. In Morocco, for example, local parents make a weighty political cultural statement by enrolling their children in these schools.

Encouraging that affinity for America should be a high priority for U.S. policy. Shockingly, however, annual U.S. assistance to American schools abroad is only about $8 million, less than 2 percent of the schools' combined $450 million operating budget. Even with the inclusion of noncash support, like tariff-free imports and corporate donations, the value of outside assistance is still a pittance.

That is especially scandalous given that American schools don't need much additional money to maximize their potential. The Rabat school, for example, has 389 students but room for another 10 percent. The main deterrent is tuition, which is a hefty $11,000, several times the local per capita income. While fees for non-Moroccans are usually paid by their parents' employer—a foreign government, multinational corporation or UN agency—Moroccan students almost always hail from wealthy families. With no endowment and very limited scholarship funds, the school lacks the means to reach out to other segments of the local population.

With an additional $200,000—or 5 percent of its budget—the school could provide half-tuition scholarships to fill the empty thirty-eight slots with local students whose families are eager to enroll their children in the American school, if they could afford it. These are middle-class Moroccans who currently scrape together the money to pay the lower tuition for other local private schools—French and Arabic—whose curriculum, to put it politely, lacks a certain appreciation for American values. If Washington were to allocate funds on that magnitude to the fifty or so accredited American schools in countries with sizable Arab or Muslim populations, that would amount to just $13.5 million.

For our family, nothing can erase the image of Benji and Muhammad standing next to each other belting out "One Little Candle." If the government can find the resources to replicate that a thousand-fold, then we will be a thousand steps closer to winning that hearts-and-minds fight.

PART IV

A New
Approach

Re-engage the World

March 2003

THE RESIGNATION OF CHARLOTTE BEERS AS UNDERSECRETARY of state for public diplomacy offers an opportunity to redirect U.S. outreach to foreign audiences away from ill-considered, feel-good therapy toward practical programs that advance our policy goals and build long-term friendships.

This is a particularly urgent task given the deepening isolation in which the United States finds itself, especially among longtime allies.

For nations liberated by America in our parents' lifetime to tell pollsters they believe that the president of the United States is a greater danger to world peace than the tyrant of Baghdad or that Americans have somehow sacrificed their moral compass while waging the war on terror bespeaks a thundering failure to deliver the message of our policies abroad.

An accomplished Madison Avenue advertising genius, Ms. Beers, who resigned Monday, never quite warmed to the prime mission of post–September 11 public diplomacy—for example, providing a robust exposition of the justice of America's cause in the war on terrorism. Main Street and the Arab Street being two very different things, the estimable skills she brought to the former were ill-suited to addressing the challenges of the latter.

The problematic result has been a public diplomacy that accentuates image over substance.

For example, much intellectual and financial capital was invested in an ill-conceived effort to burnish America's standing as a nation tolerant to Muslims in its midst. This included multimillion-dollar television ads in Asia and the Middle East, numerous speakers dispatched to spread the tolerance gos-

---

Originally published in the *Baltimore Sun*, March 9, 2003.

pel and flashy websites with smiling American Muslims, women all wearing headscarves and—here's a little secret—nary a picture of an African-American among them.

The ads were rejected by many foreign governments and even private satellite stations, who argued that tolerance was not the problem; it was disagreements over policy. But all too rarely did our public diplomacy apparatus rise to the challenge of engaging Muslim audiences directly on these policy clashes.

How can this be done? By speaking directly to people on the issues that matter, like Iraq and Israel.

On Iraq, for example, why has the State Department not organized a tour around Middle East capitals for a dozen survivors of the Halabja chemical weapons attacks so ordinary Arabs can see for themselves and hear in their own language the horror of Saddam Hussein's tyranny against his own people?

On Israel, why does our public diplomacy not speak out every day against the hate speech that passes for civil discourse in newspapers, sermons, and university lectures in many foreign countries, where the word "Zionist" is commonly understood to mean "hater of Muslims" and where Jews are routinely denounced as "sons of pigs and monkeys?"

Instead, in a self-defeating strategy to win fair-weather friends, we praise extremist clerics who, while denouncing the September 11 attacks, celebrate suicide bombings of innocents, and we channel pro-democracy funds to radical Islamist parliamentarians who use the tools they acquire to more effectively undermine the rule of our allies.

By the universal yardstick of money, public diplomacy has clearly lost the attraction it once had among the highest reaches of the administration. Indeed, President Bush's budget request for fiscal year 2004 projects a net decrease in public diplomacy spending, quite a comedown for an effort that was once viewed as the key "hearts and minds" arrow in the "war on terrorism" quiver.

The great shame is that there is so much important work to be done and so many eager, knowledgeable and creative public diplomacy veterans in government ready to do it. We should complement an unapologetic defense of our policies with long-term strategies to promote English education, boost foreign student exchange, enhance the professionalism of journalists and reward best practices by our diplomats.

Let's flood resource-poor foreign schools with books and magazines by offering U.S. publishers and shippers tax breaks to donate overruns and to deliver them overseas. Let's help local governments develop their local libraries, in their languages as well as ours, so that Middle Easterners don't have to run the security gauntlet at our fortress-like embassies to enter American Centers. Let's create incentives for U.S. corporations abroad to play greater roles in encouraging English training and high-tech education, offering the prize most highly sought by aspiring students—a job.

Let's catch up with the British and French who are light years ahead of us in advising students who want to study abroad, while we press ahead with our national system of monitoring students once they are here.

Let's establish distance-learning links between U.S. journalism schools and media programs around the world to give aspiring reporters the tools to do independent, nonpartisan, investigative journalism. And while we are making progress on this front, let's redefine the incentive structure inside our foreign service to reward ambassadors and diplomats who know local languages, speak out on local campuses and appear on local media.

As this list suggests, public diplomacy is more than just advertising. It is investing in ideas and people, so that America gets a fair hearing for its policies today and the chance to develop new allies to fight battles alongside us in the future.

How to Win Friends and
Influence Arabs

August 2003

L IKE A SPORTS TEAM AFTER A DISMAL SEASON, THE STATE
Department is going through a "rebuilding process" to figure out how to
win Arab and Muslim friends. As depressing statistics about anti-Americanism continue to mount, especially in the Middle East, Foggy Bottom recently
announced the formation of a new committee, headed by former diplomat Edward
P. Djerejian, to repair its woeful "public diplomacy" toward Arabs and Muslims.

Djerejian, head of State's Near East bureau under then-secretary James
Baker, has served for the last decade as founding director of the James A.
Baker III Institute of Public Policy at Rice University. In what could herald
a revival of Baker's team at State, Djerejian is likely to pass his committee's
findings to another Baker veteran—Margaret Tutwiler, former State spokes-
man and current ambassador to Morocco—who is expected to take over the
department's top public diplomacy job in the autumn.

Creation of Djerejian's fourteen-member panel comes four months after
the resignation of controversial public diplomacy chief Charlotte Beers, the
onetime advertising executive. Under Beers, the buzzword was "branding,"
the idea that America could earn the loyal support of customers around the
world through the sort of image-oriented campaign that wins repeat shop-
pers to Wal-Mart. Through a series of "I'm okay, you're okay" initiatives
to Muslim audiences—television commercials, websites, and speakers programs—Beers tried to reconnect the world's billion Muslims with the United
States the way McDonald's highlights its billion customers served.

The results were disastrous. Many Muslim countries refused to air the TV
spots, while many who saw them damned the ads as puerile propaganda.

Originally published in the *Weekly Standard*, August 18, 2003.

At home, complaints about the Madison Avenue approach to diplomacy grew numerous. The most definitive sign that Beers had finally lost the confidence of the White House came this year as the administration proposed a net decrease in State Department spending on public diplomacy, despite the universally recognized need to improve America's message abroad. Beers resigned on March 3.

Not everyone agrees on the reasons for Beers's failure. The Djerejian committee will hear three different analyses. Each one portends a wholly different approach to public diplomacy.

One view holds that Beers was right to focus on common values (such as family, home, religion) and cultural interests (pop music, sports) that Americans share with foreign Muslims, but that she was too tentative and cautious in pressing the case. Advocates of this view—such as proponents of the new U.S. government-funded Arabic radio and satellite television networks—believe that blitzing Arab and Muslim countries with Britney Spears videos and Arabic-language sitcoms will earn Washington millions of new Muslim sympathizers.

A second view holds that many Muslims hate us for who we are, so unless we are going to change our spots, we should stop worrying about Muslim sensibilities altogether. Washington is the new Rome, these realpoliticians say, and an imperial power—even a benign one—should focus its energies on efficiency, not popularity. The only public diplomacy that matters, this argument goes, comes with victory (over al-Qaeda, the Taliban, Saddam, etc.).

A third view holds that Muslims hate us for what we do, not who we are, and counsels that we must change our policies if we hope to restore some luster to America's standing. Adherents—mostly critics of current U.S. Middle East policy—urge Washington to distance itself from Israel, get out of Iraq, and abandon President Bush's revolutionary talk about promoting freedom in Iran.

If Djerejian's panel is smart, it will reject all three approaches.

Yes, many Muslims do disagree with aspects of our Middle East policy, but selling out our friends, like Israel, to suit our critics is just an invitation to blackmail.

Yes, winning the war on terror is vital for U.S. security, but our anti-terror campaign will require local partners to ensure that the terrorists are on the run, not just underground.

And yes, values matter, but most Muslims aren't teeny-boppers who can be swayed by a rap artist from the 'hood who extols the virtues of Islam. Incidentally, the State Department really does spend tax money on promoting a

Muslim rap group, Native Deen, whose lead singer, Joshua Salaam, is civil rights director for the Hamas-friendly Council for American-Islamic Relations. Salaam once praised the terrorists who blew up the USS Cole for having "a lot of guts to attack the United States military." Very ironic, of course, as is the fact that Salaam himself served four years in the U.S. Air Force.

How, then, should the job of promoting American interests be approached? The first step is to recognize that a successful public diplomacy relies on three ingredients: a short-term focus on image, a long-term investment in future allies, and, most of all, a consistent emphasis on promoting U.S. interests.

Advancing U.S. policies must be the touchstone of all public diplomacy. Sounds obvious, but it is actually a radical statement, completely out of touch with the State Department's feel-good outreach to Arabs and Muslims over the past two years. In the post–September 11 world, we help neither ourselves nor the millions of moderate Muslims around the world by substituting serious talk about the dangers of militant Islam with dumbed-down, Rodney King-style patter about everyone "getting along."

It is true that many Muslims disagree with U.S. policies, but what they know often comes from the distorted, caricatured view of reality propagated by irresponsible local media prevalent in most Muslim countries. Those media have a field day with U.S. policy because most U.S. officials rarely talk to them—adult to adult—about what our views really are and why we hold them. For example: Despite the fact that the FBI's most wanted terrorist list includes three Hizballah operatives responsible for the 1983 bombings of the U.S. embassy in Beirut, the current U.S. ambassador in Lebanon closed his remarks at the solemn ceremony marking the twentieth anniversary of that heinous act of terrorism by extolling the power of "forgiveness." One hardly wants to know who he thinks is supposed to forgive whom?

With rare exceptions, such as David Welch in Egypt and Ronald Neumann in Bahrain, U.S. officials in the Arab world hardly ever take the trouble to explain to local audiences, plainly and dispassionately, why Americans support Israel, oppose militant Islam, and feared Saddam Hussein. *[Editor's note: In 2004, Neumann gave up his ambassadorial position in Bahrain to become head of political-military affairs at the U.S. embassy in Baghdad, the post's third-ranking position.]* But the U.S. government, in an odd effort to promote Arab contributions toward Middle East peace, did spend thousands of dollars last month broadcasting and distributing a program on its international television network that suggested the way to achieve progress was to "pressure Israel." This is cockeyed.

Polishing America's image is a key element of public diplomacy too, but only if it is imbued with purpose. One example of a failure waiting to happen is the U.S. government's new Arabic language radio station, Sawa.

In 2002, Sawa became the darling of Capitol Hill based on a listener poll showing that it had won a large audience in several Arab countries through an innovative mix of pop and Arabic music, interspersed with brief, informative, U.S.-style news reports. But Sawa's braintrust rested on these flimsy laurels, opting not to beef up its content with significantly more news, analysis, and talk. (Instead, it heralded further listener poll numbers that its news content was "just right.") The result is that Sawa is on the verge of becoming just another radio station, easily replicable, instead of something uniquely American.

Arab and Muslim leaders aren't stupid. They may not have devised Sawa's music mix, but they know how to copy it. Last month, Jordanian army radio launched its own new station based on the pop-Arabic music format; Morocco already has a station with this cross-cultural mix; others are sure to follow. So unless Sawa begins to provide its listeners with a message they will never get from local radio stations, it is doomed.

Getting the questions of interests and image right is not enough. Unless our public diplomacy is reoriented to support our friends, isolate our critics, and punish our adversaries it will remain part of America's problem abroad, not part of the solution. Sadly, much of what we do today is just the opposite.

Instead of investing money and effort to help millions of secular, liberal Muslims who fear the spread of Wahhabi radicalism, we spend our time searching under every rock for elusive "moderate Islamists." Incredible as it sounds, the U.S. government also spends tax dollars to subsidize study visits to the United States by radical Islamist journalists, to send outspoken critics of U.S. policy on speaking tours abroad, and to teach anti-American Islamist parliamentarians how to criticize pro-Western governments more effectively.

Every dime spent on such masochistic folly should instead go to investing in our local allies, the brave men and women who fight the daily battle to educate their kids and raise wholesome families in the face of rising religious totalitarianism. This means encouraging American businesses abroad to adopt local schools and support technical training, pumping up the pittance we spend on English-language education, and targeting our exchange programs to reward our current friends and identify future ones. Washington has begun to get some things right, such as restarting Arabic-language publishing after a decade in which all print ventures were scrapped in favor of Internet-based outreach—a silly idea given that the Middle East is the world's least-linked region of the world. But it is far too little and much too late.

Three principles—promoting our interests, investing in allies, and advancing a principled image of ourselves—should form the core of America's redesigned public diplomacy. Of course, even if we do all this, we may never win popularity contests in Cairo or Casablanca. But if Djerejian and company get it right, then at least our soldiers and our public diplomacy specialists will be fighting on the same side.

The Djerejian Report: An Assessment

October 2003

I N ITS EIGHTY-PAGE REPORT "CHANGING MINDS, WINNING
Peace," issued earlier today, the State Department's Advisory Group on
Public Diplomacy for the Arab and Muslim World—chaired by Edward
Djerejian—delivered a refreshingly blunt assessment of many of the failures
in Washington's efforts to deliver its message to Muslims worldwide, offering
a series of generally useful, often innovative, and sometimes audacious suggestions. The report's main flaws, however, are its silence on radical Islamism
as the core "hearts and minds" challenge to U.S. interests in the region under
review; its implicit emphasis on poll-driven initiatives; its lack of prioritization in offering numerous new initiatives; and a disconcerting tendency
toward institutional "special pleading."

Headlines

The following are the report's most significant recommendations:

- Demonstrate presidential commitment to a new "strategic direction" for
  public diplomacy, which would not only recognize the importance that
  public diplomacy plays in U.S. national security, but also reinforce that
  recognition with resources, personnel, and ongoing presidential interest.

- Initiate a thorough overhaul of the bureaucratic design of U.S. public diplomacy, including the creation of a presidential "counselor," the invigoration

Originally published as *PolicyWatch* number 788, October 1, 2003.

of the National Security Council/Principals Coordinating Committee on public diplomacy, the formation of a Public Diplomacy Experts Board, the establishment of a government-chartered Corporation of Public Diplomacy, and the funding of a Center for U.S.-Arab/Muslim Studies and Dialogue.

- Budget significant new funding for a broad array of public diplomacy initiatives, including additional personnel and training; academic and professional exchanges; improved and expanded use of information technology; and investment in English-language training, new "American Knowledge Libraries," and book translation and American studies opportunities at foreign universities throughout the Arab and Muslim worlds.

Attacking Sacred Cows

Some of the most important passages of the report are critiques of existing programs. While the drafters are careful to couch their comments in constructive, nonthreatening language, their arguments are clear. Three programs are given special scrutiny:

- **Radio Sawa and the proposed new Middle East Television Network.** The report is perhaps most valuable for injecting some much-needed sanity into the Washington debate over new radio and television stations targeted at Middle East audiences. In pointed criticism of the current market-driven strategy of Radio Sawa, which replaced Voice of America's Arabic service last year, the report states, "Sawa needs a clearer objective than building a large audience. . . . Indeed, we worry that the [Broadcasting Board of Governors'] nearly single-minded objective for Sawa is audience-building—a target that may deter Sawa from adding more influential content." Regarding television, the report is even more critical, suggesting that the entire project be chucked: "An attractive, less costly alternative or supplement to METN may be the aggressive development of programming in partnership with private firms. . . ." In bureaucratic terms, this is a strong vote of no confidence in the Broadcasting Board of Governors.

- **U.S. speaker programs abroad.** While reaffirming the wisdom of sending hundreds of nongovernmental experts overseas to inform foreign audiences about aspects of U.S. policy, culture, and society, the report cited three new tests that such programs should pass before they receive support. The fact that the report's drafters felt compelled to note that speakers should pass the political "smell test"—i.e., "How can this speaker help improve attitudes toward the United States?"—underscores how little vetting has gone on in such programs in the past.

- **Middle East study centers.** There is much to debate about the report's proposal to create a national Center for U.S.-Arab/Muslim Studies and Dialogue (e.g., where Israel fits in the mix; the counterproductive effect of lumping countries as disparate as Nigeria, Syria, Indonesia, and Uzbekistan into a single research institute based on common religion). Yet, the fact that the Djerejian committee saw the need for a new government-funded undertaking is further proof that existing government-funded Middle East resource centers at universities around the country are not fulfilling the critical needs outlined in the report.

A Common-Sense Approach

In practical terms, the Djerejian committee has provided a useful service by endorsing many needed improvements in the way the State Department engages in public diplomacy (e.g., more language and media education) and by pointing out areas deserving of investment (especially publishing and English-language education). In this regard, changing the culture of public diplomacy, providing incentives for innovation, and weaving public diplomacy into regional bureaus are all essential. In addition, the report cited the important role to be played by public-private partnerships in public diplomacy, including cooperation with the business sector, universities, and non-governmental organizations.

Problems

Although many of the report's proposals deserve support, the Djerejian committee regrettably sidestepped several key, fundamental issues:

- **The challenge of radical Islamism.** The most significant lacuna in the report is its failure to identify clearly radical Islam as the main "hearts and minds" challenge in the Muslim world. Instead, the report offers an ide-ology-blind definition of the challenge: "The solutions that we advocate match these times, when we are engaged in a major, long-term struggle against the forces of extremism, whether secular or religious." Surely the authors of this report know that secular extremism neither fuels the war on terror nor funds anti-Americanism at thousands of madrasas, universities, and children's summer camps around the Arab and Muslim worlds. With-out clear identification of the challenge, there can be no serious discussion of the appropriate content for broadcasting, targets for exchanges, or top-ics for translation, virtually none of which are discussed in the report.

- **An over-reliance on poll-driven public diplomacy.** The report makes a game effort at addressing one problem—the lack of efforts to measure effectiveness in current programming—but its emphasis on audience test-ing and poll taking as the main solution would only replace one problem with another. The drafters appear to want it both ways—i.e., to support a long-term approach of nurturing future allies through exchanges and education, and to secure fast, measurable results that would show up in the next round of Pew polls on foreign public opinion. Indeed, the very concept of "changing minds" suggests a focus on polls rather than on the need to build constituencies. A more courageous report would have bluntly urged U.S. officials to disregard polls except for measuring long-term trends.

- **A lack of prioritization.** Like virtually all other reports on public diplo-macy, the Djerejian report focuses on the need for more funding. Calling for additional funds is the easy part. What is missing is a sense of priority and urgency—what should be funded more in the short term (e.g., print publishing versus internet outreach) and what could be cut. Other than a useful suggestion to review spending on international broadcasting, the report does not seem to offer any clues regarding new funding priorities. In this regard, the report missed an opportunity to be particularly helpful to the body that chartered it, the House Committee on Appropriations.

- **Special pleading for Foggy Bottom.** The report's executive summary exonerates the State Department and its personnel of all responsibility for the woeful state of public diplomacy: "The fault lies not with the dedi-cated men and women at the State Department and elsewhere who practice public diplomacy . . . but with a system that has become outmoded." This is a whitewash. While it is true that there are hundreds of valued, creative, and patriotic public diplomacy professionals in Foggy Bottom and at posts around the globe, it is also true that America's public diplomacy has suffered by short-sighted, politically correct, and counterproductive decisions taken by public diplomacy offsicials. Given the central role played in drafting the report by members of the existing State Department public diplomacy team, it is perhaps too much to have expected direct criticism. Yet, giving a blanket amnesty to every member of that team undermines the seriousness with which the report addresses other issues.

A Practical Guide to Tapping America's Underappreciated, Underutilized Anti-Islamist Allies

August 2004

WITH MORE THAN 1.3 BILLION MUSLIMS WORLDWIDE, it is not realistic for the United States government—working both independently and in concert with other governments, international organizations, and private initiatives—to thoroughly "drain the swamp" in which Islamist[1] terrorist organizations find their recruits. Even if one were to accept a low-end estimate of the number of Islamists worldwide (say, 5 percent of all Muslims) and a low-end estimate of the number of terrorists or their activist sympathizers—financiers, logistical supporters, ideological advocates—among them (say, 1 percent of all Islamists), then there are at least 600,000 hard-core radicals fishing for followers in a sea of at least 60,000,000 potential recruits.[2] To identify, target, isolate, co-opt, and, in some cases, neutralize the former is a gargantuan task. To do the same to the latter is patently impossible.

If fully "draining the swamp" is not achievable, however, there remains much that can be done to decrease the number of Muslims who become Islamists and to decrease the number of Islamists who become terrorists or their activist sympathizers. Each of these challenges requires different tools and different strategies. In essence, whereas decreasing the number of Islamists who become terrorists is principally the province of intelligence and security agencies, decreasing the number of Muslims who become Islamists is a much wider concern that touches on numerous aspects of U.S. foreign policy.

Curtailing the appeal of Islamism should be a matter of prime importance to practitioners of what is popularly known as "public diplomacy." To many, public diplomacy is merely a less grating term for "public relations abroad,"

Excerpted from *A Practical Guide to Winning the War on Terrorism*, ed. Adam Garfinkle (Hoover Institution Press, 2004), pp. 181–194. Reprinted with permission.

or the less-than-fine-art of packaging and selling America to foreign audiences. Although that is an element of the larger picture, public diplomacy is—or *ought* to be—much more than that.

Just as traditional diplomacy revolves around strengthening allies, weakening adversaries, and advancing America's interests and values, the same can be said of public diplomacy. Although the targets are different (peoples, not government) and the operational time frame is often longer, the objectives are similar: empowering friends, undermining the influence of adversaries, and nurturing popular understanding of (and, one hopes, support for) U.S. national interests and values. Unfortunately, too few professional public diplomats view their mission in terms of allies and adversaries. Indeed, the fundamental problem of U.S. public diplomacy in the post–September 11 era is that it has rarely evinced a clear sense of mission, has rarely differentiated clearly between friend and foe, and has rarely focused its energies on extending a helping hand to those elements in society—especially in Muslim-majority countries—that are America's natural allies in the struggle against radical Islamism.

Defining a detailed, full-scale, soup-to-nuts program to achieve those objectives is beyond the scope of this brief essay. However, what follows are three broad suggestions that, if implemented, would begin to put U.S. public diplomacy squarely on the right side of the fight against Islamism.

Identifying and Supporting Allies

As noted above, the overwhelming majority of the world's Muslims are not Islamists. However, Islamists are often highly motivated and well funded. Although they are not choreographed by some all-knowing Islamist wizard, they coordinate well among themselves and (especially the nonviolent ones) have a sophisticated, long-range plan to advance their goals. They are people of action. In contrast, non-Islamist Muslims are defined more by who they are *not* rather than by who they are. They range across political and religious spectra, from radical atheists to secular, lapsed Muslims to pious, traditional, orthodox believers. They have no common program, no organizational cohesion, no way even to know who in society shares their views.

An important, and rarely pursued, step toward minimizing recruits to Islamism is to identify the potential allies among these non-Islamist Muslims, build networks of common purpose among them, and show that the United

States supports them in the currency that matters in local society—that is, visibility and money.

This task requires a different sort of outreach effort than is the norm for U.S. embassies in the Muslim world. Rather than seek out "moderate Islamists" for dialogue designed to promote understanding of U.S. policies and to narrow differences over contested issues, this alternative approach would have U.S. embassies pointedly avoid contact with Islamists (except for intelligence gathering). Instead, it highlights contacts with liberal, even secular, anti-Islamist individuals and organizations. Invitations to embassy functions, participation in ambassadorial press conferences, and opportunities for exchange visits and study tours to the United States are all ways for U.S. officials to shower favor upon groups and individuals. These actions should be viewed as arrows in the larger public diplomacy quiver, for even in this era of pessimistic Pew Research Center polls of America's standing abroad, the imprimatur of the United States is sorely coveted. So are the dollars that U.S. governmental agencies and quasi-official nongovernmental organizations (like the National Endowment for Democracy's recipient agencies) dole out to local groups.

In all these programs, the guiding principle should be that the United States supports its current friends and would welcome new ones. Local political communities around the Muslim world are sophisticated: when they see that anti-Islamists of varying stripes (whether female entrepreneurs, crusading investigative journalists, or kids who win English-language spelling bees) are featured at embassy events, receive embassy grants, and win trips to the United States—with nary an Islamist among them—the message will be clear. Conversely, a clear and damaging message is transmitted when Islamists, even of the mild variety, are the honored guests, lucky beneficiaries, and welcome visitors on those events, grants, and trips.

In addition to highlighting contact with cultural and political allies, U.S. embassies abroad and U.S. public diplomacy in general should focus efforts on networking among groups and individuals that, at least on the Islamist issue, share a common approach. Like building a popular front against Nazism in World War II or against Communism in the Cold War, this may involve bringing together people of very different worldviews to work together for the larger cause of fighting the spread of Islamism. Ironically, U.S. officials who either shun "secularists" for fear of offending Muslim sensibilities, or who have little expertise in distinguishing between traditionalist Muslims and Islamists, are more likely to be reluctant to adopt this approach than are local anti-Islamist Muslims themselves. Because the latter are on the "front line," facing the rising tide of Islamism in schools, mosques, youth groups, grassroots organizations, and civic groups, they are more likely to take risks. The United States should not leave such allies and potential allies out in the cold.

Building such networks is not only important for creating a force-multiplier of reformist activism to counter the Islamists, it is also useful for identifying individuals who could play lead roles in specific public policy issues. Curriculum reform, for example, is a critical battleground of the culture wars in many Muslim societies. The traditional U.S. approach is to offer technical assistance to ministries of education (in the form of consultants, study trips to the United States, the professional advice of English-language officers at embassies, and so forth). However, these efforts periodically fuel criticism and resentment toward U.S. interference in one of the most sensitive areas of local concern.

A more effective and longer-lasting change—and one with fewer fingerprints of U.S. intervention—would result from behind-the-scenes U.S. endorsement of key reform-minded people from within the bureaucracy and civil society to positions of authority on the local and national review boards often formed to review curricula. Trying to influence the composition of various government bodies both removes the United States from direct interference in the actual process of curriculum reform and ensures that right-thinking people will be in important positions when the current battle is over and the next one is ready to be joined. This can only be achieved if U.S. embassies have already done the vital work of identifying local allies and building a communications infrastructure for networking among them.

Empowering Allies

Although lending visible political support to anti-Islamists is essential, it is not sufficient. The U.S. government should also find innovative ways to strengthen its local anti-Islamist allies. One critical, yet low-cost, arena in which the United States can empower anti-Islamists is in the information field.

One of the lesser-known phenomena in Arab and Muslim society in recent years is the flowering of nongovernmental organizations (NGOs). From remote mountainous regions in the High Atlas to the urban slums of Cairo, these organizations have sprouted up to fulfill all sorts of communal and social needs. Sometimes they emerge from the commitment of local community organizers. Sometimes they are creatures of the government, which may construct ad hoc local groups to perform special functions or fulfill services that the government chooses to channel outside the formal system. Sometimes they are local branches of organizations that have large, international followings.

Whatever their origins, tens of thousands of these organizations now exist throughout the Middle East, and a large number of them are Islamist in orientation. Many of these are registered with local governments in accordance with law, but many others operate in a legal vacuum. In a region where the central government's delivery of basic social services is notoriously bad, NGOs have emerged in many places to supply what governments either cannot or do not provide. Of course, Islamist organizations only compensate for a small fraction of what governments are not able or willing to do, but the model they offer still provides a pathway for the spread of Islamist thought and, possibly, terrorist sympathies to millions of Muslims.

Throughout Arab and Muslim countries, for example, Islamist NGOs—many financed from Saudi Arabia, some with al-Qaeda links—have established powerful networks of Islamist-oriented social welfare initiatives. Following a long-term strategy of nurturing the next generation of Islamists, some of the most insidious Islamist NGOs focus exclusively on children. (Hence, for example, they might opt to fund primary schools, youth camps, and after-school programming but not current needs of the adult population, such as adult literacy programs, vocational training classes, or battered women's shelters.) Often, these NGOs operate without formal government license because their services often fill a local need. Local administrators often either look the other way or welcome these organizations, regardless of what officialdom in faraway capitals might prefer (or say they prefer).

Among anti-Islamists, even without knowing about the shadier international links of many of these groups, there is a rising sense of alarm at the spread of such Islamist social welfare activities. Many civic activists, including journalists, would take up the cudgel against the presence of these foreign-funded Islamist organizations and would be especially moved to act if they knew about the possible terrorist connections of some of these outfits. What these activists lack, however, is information, such as documentary evidence describing the political activities and funding sources of these groups and, when it exists, evidence of connection to terrorist acts and organizations. Such information is, to a large extent, part of the U.S. public record, from court transcripts, FBI documents, and congressional reports and testimonies. Indeed, the Treasury Department's Office of Foreign Asset Control publishes a list of "specially designated nationals and blocked persons" that, in the version of September 23, 2003, is 116 pages long. Many of the institutions cited on this list are the same Islamist NGOs that are active in many corners of the Muslim world.[3]

A simple, low-cost but high-value solution would be the creation of a user-friendly, Internet-based clearinghouse of information in Arabic and other local languages, outlining the operations, management, administration, financing, and personnel of all Islamist-oriented initiatives and NGOs and the linkages among them. Such an effort, if brought to the attention of the growing number of anti-Islamist activists and organizations through an aggressive, imaginative outreach campaign, would be a forceful stimulant to action. Information is power, and this sort of information would help empower anti-Islamist Muslims who are concerned about the direction of their own countries and communities to take matters into their own hands.

Nurturing Future Allies

In the campaign to limit the spread of Islamism, identifying, supporting, and empowering current allies is necessary but still not sufficient. To stand any chance of undercutting the Islamists' popular appeal, the United States must invest much more substantially in developing new and future allies. Here, a central battleground is children's education. Indeed, this is one area in which anti-Islamists should take their cue from Islamists, who, as noted above, have made the battle for the "hearts and minds" of young people a top priority. So far, the United States is not even putting up a fight.

In approaching this problem, it is important to remember another lesson learned from the Islamists: the power of example. In the context of populous countries like Egypt, Morocco, Algeria, and Yemen, Islamist social welfare programming is a proverbial drop in the bucket compared with what actual needs are, and even compared with what existing governments currently do. In a medium-sized town, for example, Islamists may successfully operate a model school, a professionally staffed hospital, or a well-functioning day-care center, but they cannot replace the government's massive, though admittedly broken-down, educational or health care systems. Like terrorists who have learned the ways of asymmetric warfare against conventional armies, Islamists have mastered the tools of reaping considerable public sympathy from providing examples of a better-run alternative system without having the responsibility or burden of actually providing such an alternative system.

Curtailing the popular appeal of Islamism should be pursued with a similar strategy. Although the U.S. government can provide some assistance to help fix local school systems, the problems are too huge—and the Islamist challenge is too urgent—to rely on that approach. Instead, Washington needs to develop alternative opportunities for anti-Islamist excellence and highly visible models of it.

Promoting English-language education should be a central focus of this effort. Knowing English does not necessarily translate into liberal thought or pro-Americanism, as the legacy of Islamist radicals from Sayyid Qutb to the September 11 bombers underscores. But English is both a portal to Anglo-American culture as well as the access route to the Internet-based information revolution. Knowing English at least gives a resident in a Muslim-majority country the opportunity to learn about America and make judgments about its policies and values without the filter of translation or reliance on biased sources of information. Indeed, studies show that access to information is not itself the key criterion in shaping views on U.S. policy; rather, it is access to different sorts and sources of information—for example, CNN versus al-Jazeera—that could be the key to determining attitudes toward the United States.[4]

Specific initiatives that could be pursued in this strategy include the following:

- Create "English-for-all" after-school programs, at no or nominal cost to parents, in cities and towns throughout the Muslim world. This should be pursued cooperatively with existing NGOs as well as with the governments of other English-speaking countries and the English Speaking Union, the British-based organization that seeks to promote the use of the English language around the globe. Similarly, U.S. funds should subsidize the high fees that older students are currently asked to pay for English-language training at specialized programs like AMIDEAST, thereby making those classes more accessible to a wider segment of the population. Few steps could earn the United States more goodwill in Muslim countries than to invest enough money to make English-language study free or extremely low-cost.

- Expand the existing paltry financial support for American-style educational opportunities for students of all ages throughout the Muslim world. Of the 185 U.S. government–recognized "American schools" around the world, fully one-quarter are in Muslim-majority countries and one-tenth are in Arab countries.[5] These schools—readymade incubators of pro-Americanism—receive paltry levels of assistance from the U.S. government, only $8 million out of a combined annual operating budget of $450 million. Some schools receive as little as 1 percent of their annual operating budget from government funds. Many of these schools attract high concentrations—one-third to one-half—of local students but their often five-digit tuition fees mean that only wealthy, elite local children can attend, sometimes without regard to academic excellence. (Tuition fees for most other students are paid for by governments and international corporations.) Washington should target schools in Arab and Muslim countries for expanded merit-based, academic scholarship funds. These would help to expand the pool of local entrants and to reach beyond "old money" families to the rising middle class who yearn for a U.S.-style education and who are willing to pay substantial sums for it, but who cannot afford the exorbitant costs that cash-strapped schools are forced to charge to make ends meet.

- Support the development of U.S.-style universities throughout the Muslim world through enhanced distance-learning facilities, provision of books and supplies, educational training grants, and the like. The long-term goal should be the creation of at least one fully accredited English-language university in every country. The fact that new, U.S.-style, English-language universities are opening throughout the Muslim world—Kuwait's is the most recent, scheduled to begin instruction in September 2004—is a trend to be embraced and cultivated. Given the heightened security concerns about foreign students in the United States, combined with a financial crunch that forced a cutback in foreign Muslim and Arab students in the United States well before September 11, promoting U.S.-style universities in Muslim countries is an especially smart idea.

- Promote the distribution in Muslim countries of overstock U.S. textbooks and academic materials. Current law provides for tax breaks for book publishers to donate overstocks, but the number of books that make their way to Arab or Muslim countries is shockingly low.[6]

- Integrate the U.S. private sector, especially U.S. companies operating abroad, in English-language promotion. This could range from developing incentive programs that promise postgraduation employment for students who complete certain coursework or technical training to providing tax incentives to corporations that provide financial support to book-purchasing initiatives, English-language programs, or scholarship funds in their local overseas communities.

Even a long list of initiatives such as this (and the list could be much longer) will only touch a relatively small number of students at all ages. But just as Islamists enjoy a reputation for providing efficient social welfare services far beyond the actual reach of people that receive such services, so, too, will the example of successful English-language programming attract admirers far beyond the actual number of students that directly benefit from it. And along the way, the United States will have invested in the next generation of Muslim allies to carry on the campaign to limit the appeal of Islamism.

A Diplomacy of Doing

There is a tendency to see public diplomacy as mainly talking: whether through radio broadcasts, speaker programs, or print publications and the like. That is about as inadequate a view of public diplomacy as demarching foreign governments is of traditional diplomacy. To be effective, public diplomacy requires action—assertive, aggressive, creative efforts to engage foreign publics, nurture friends, empower allies, build future supporters, and undercut the leverage of America's adversaries. To succeed against as wily and sophisticated a challenge as Islamism requires resorting to means not usually the hallmark of traditional diplomacy. These means include more public-private partnerships, for example, and the encouragement of a more entrepreneurial, risk-taking, opportunistic, and decentralized way of doing business by America's embassies and diplomats.

This, in turn, will require changes from the current pattern of foreign service recruitment, education, training, and placement. Indeed, to a great extent, a successful public diplomacy campaign against Islamism means a throwback to the days before all diplomacy was directed from Washington, to the era when embassies and diplomats were active, frontline agents in the advance of American national interests. Only a diplomatic corps imbued with mission, charged with action, and unleashed from bureaucracy can win the friends and allies America needs to triumph in the battle to curtail the appeal of Islamism.

Notes

1. Islamist is defined here as a Muslim who seeks—either through peaceful or violent means—the imposition of Qur'anic law (Sharia) and a Qur'anic-based state, rejecting the legitimacy of the existing political structure in his/her country or region. Although organically antidemocratic (i.e., opposed to "rule of the people"), Islamists can equally reject democratic systems and monarchical ones, the principal point of departure for them being the imperative to impose "divine law" in place of human-made systems of governance.

2. Daniel Pipes, for example, suggests that "perhaps 10 to 15 percent" of all Muslims subscribe to "militant Islam." See Pipes, *Militant Islam Reaches America* (New York: W.W. Norton, 2002), 3.

3. For the OFAC list, periodically updated, see http://www.treas.org/office/eotffc/ofac/sdn/t11sdn.pdf. *[Editor's note: The aforementioned link is no longer valid. As of September 2004, the correct link for the OFAC list, now updated, is www.ustreas.gov/offices/enforcement/ofac/sdn/t11sdn.pdf]*

4. See Matthew A. Gentzkow and Jesse M. Shapiro, "Education, Media and Anti-Americanism in the Muslim World," a study by two Harvard University students based on data from the 2002 Gallup poll of the Islamic World, http://www.people.fas.harvard.edu/~jmshapir/summary100303.pdf.

5. For details on American schools around the world, see the Web site of the U.S. State Department's Office of Overseas Schools, http://www.state.gov/m/a/os/.

6. For details of tax exemptions and one overseas book-distribution program, see the Sabre Foundation, http://www.sabre.org.

Private Initiatives and
Public Diplomacy

June 2004

T HE IMPORTANCE OF PURSUING POLITICAL, SOCIAL, AND economic reform in the region now frequently described as the "Broader Middle East and North Africa" is no longer in doubt. While it is legitimate to debate the wisdom of past efforts at securing elusive "regional stability" by tolerating or even supporting Arab and Muslim autocrats, there is now wide consensus that maintaining such a policy, while paying only periodic and superficial attention to the issues of freedom, democracy, and human rights, is no longer in the best interests of the United States. Remarkably, this view is now widely held among the U.S. political elite[1] and even shared by some of America's European allies, including nations that opposed the Iraq war.[2]

That such a wide array of Western leaders has reached this conclusion is not a self-evident product of the September 11 attacks and the subsequent war on terrorism. A compelling argument could be made that effective counterterrorism efforts—of the sort needed to win the battle against a network of terrorist groups as amorphous, sophisticated, decentralized, nimble, and sly as al-Qaeda and its affiliates—requires strengthening the powers and reach of central governments in Arab and Muslim countries, especially their security services. Indeed, one could argue that, at least in the short run, more authoritarianism—not less—is essential to defeat the jihadists.

To their credit, after an initial focus on fostering counterterrorism cooperation, the United States and many of its allies did not accept an authoritarian approach, although numerous Arab and Muslim leaders did try to make a case for it. Instead, they accepted a different logic: that the negative repercus-

Previously unpublished essay.

sions of jihadists deriving succor, popularity, and recruits from societies that lack healthy and vibrant social, economic, and political systems are greater than the short-term benefits of strengthening local autocrats in their fight against the radicals.

To a certain extent, this is because the recent past suggests that the eagerness of local rulers to combat Islamic extremists often stops at their international borders; even domestically, it is frequently limited to the most violent fringe, giving the less violent (though no less incendiary) extremists wide berth to operate in local politics and civil society. In other words, exporting jihad and tolerating nonviolent extremism has been, for some, an acceptable policy. The high cost borne by the United States and other Western nations for this policy—exemplified by, but not limited to, the September 11 attacks—was the trigger for a fundamental rethinking of their relations with Arab and Muslim states. Though the specific shape of policies is still under debate, the principle that emerged from this reconsideration of strategy is that the health, vibrancy, and legitimacy of domestic social, economic, and political systems in Arab and Muslim states—once viewed solely through the "soft" prisms of humanitarian objectives and human rights—are now valid national security concerns.

Complexity and Enormity: The Parameters of Reform in the "Broader Middle East"

Before considering ways to translate that core idea into practical policies, it is important to appreciate the complexity and enormity of the task. As defined by the Bush administration, the Broader Middle East includes an area comprising twenty-seven countries—all twenty-two member-states of the Arab League plus non-Arab Turkey, Iran, Pakistan, Afghanistan, and Israel. This swath of the globe—from the Atlantic coast to the depths of Central Asia, from the gates of Europe to the Sahara Desert—includes more than a half-billion people.

Although more than 95 percent are Muslim, including virtually all the world's native Arabic speakers, the area still includes a wide array of ethnic, linguistic, and subreligious groupings. A surprisingly low percentage—much less than half and perhaps only about one-third—of the people of this region speak Arabic as their native tongue. Such is the case even with the area commonly referred to as the "Arab world," a quarter of whose inhabitants do not claim Arabic as their first language (or even language of choice); these include millions of Kurds, Berbers, and Turkmens, people who define themselves ethnically as non-Arabs. Though all the countries in the region—except the special case of Israel—have Muslim majorities, many include sizable non-Muslim minorities, especially Alawites, Druze, Copts, Assyrians, and other Christians. Even the Muslim majorities are not uniform, with Shiite-majority or plurality states like Iran, Iraq, Lebanon, and Bahrain, as well as Sunni states with significant Shiite minorities like Saudi Arabia, Pakistan, and Kuwait. For its part, Israel has a sizable Sunni Arab minority within a majority Jewish population. (When one includes territory under Israeli military rule, those two populations are, for all intents and purposes, demographically equal in size.)

Politically, the region is a salad bowl of political systems and strategic alliances. It includes two fully developed, though still young, democracies (Turkey and Israel); a handful of rule-not-reign monarchies, all pursuing reform agendas of various sorts (Morocco, Jordan, and certain Gulf countries); anti-Islamist, authoritarian military regimes, often dressed in parliamentary garb, that are strategically aligned with the West (Egypt, Pakistan, Yemen, Algeria, and Tunisia); failed revolutionary regimes still seeking their way in the post–Cold War, post–September 11 world (Syria, Libya, and Sudan); and the odd case of Iran, an Islamist revolution gone sour and regressing even further into isolation. And then there are the special cases of Afghanistan, Iraq, Somalia, and the Palestinian Authority. The first two of these suffered grievously under totalitarian regimes that were overthrown by U.S. and allied forces and are now going through the painful process of being rebuilt from the bottom up; the second two are themselves failed or failing entities, crumbling under the watchful and malevolent gaze of the local leadership.

Looked at as a whole, the dominant characteristic of this region is contrast, not uniformity or even complementarity. It is very much a region of individual states, each with its own local histories, cultures, and politics. While it is now de rigueur to issue caveats against "one size fits all" strategies of reform, it is no less important to dispense with even using terminology that propagates the fallacy that ethnic, linguistic, or religious bonds in this region trump national affiliations. Not only do the concepts of "Arab world" or "Muslim world" lack relevance, they should, in fact, be banished from the policy lexicon because their use plays into the hands of the Islamists.

Championing the state, as opposed to suprastatal concepts of "Arab world" or "Muslim world," is a key element in the fight against Islamism.

Islamists, after all, have declared as one of their main goals the destruction of nation-states, which they consider bastard creations of European colonial border demarcations and local quislings. In their place, many Islamists urge the re-creation of the "caliphate"—the post-Muhammad rule of righteously guided politico-religious figures, the last vestige of which was effaced by Kemal Ataturk in the early 1920s—and the transformation of the *umma* (the worldwide Muslim community) into the unit of Muslim political activity. Indeed, the transnational networking of Islamist groupings—evidenced in terrorist plots like those that targeted New York and Madrid, as well as in ideological movements like the Muslim Brotherhood—should be viewed as one manifestation of this suprastatal effort.

Statements, programs, and policies defined to counter the spread of Islamism should not feed into this effort by ceding the political or ideological high ground to the jihadists. To the contrary, anti-Islamist initiatives must be focused locally and on individual states, eschewing as much as possible the rhetoric of "regions" to which Arabs or Muslims might owe allegiance separate and apart from their home country. (In this regard, the otherwise inelegant term "Broader Middle East" does have a certain benefit, since it is a geography-based term of Western origin that Islamists would deride as anti-Islamic and would never adopt as their own.)

If the complexity of defining policies for a set of countries so diverse is daunting, so is the enormity of the task. Promoting the reform of Arab and Muslim countries stands a good chance of emerging as the defining principle of international politics in the post–Cold War era, just as the battle between Western liberal capitalism and Soviet communism animated international politics for the second half of the twentieth century. But here the task is, in many ways, much more difficult than the one faced by two generations of cold warriors.

On the military front, the Cold War saw skirmishes throughout the globe (in Latin America, East and Southeast Asia, and elsewhere), but the main front was in Central Europe. With the Islamists, the front moves swiftly from New York to Afghanistan to Iraq to Madrid and has no central focus. Against the Soviets, the West (especially the United States) could, over time, wear down its opponents' will and ability through sheer military superiority. Against the Islamists, the option of asymmetric warfare obviates much of the benefit of traditional military power (though only through the use of such power can safe havens, such as Afghanistan under the Taliban, be effectively eliminated). Ideologically, communism was an alternative system that could only gain adherents if putative supporters were shielded from learning about the West; once cracks emerged in the proverbial wall, the entire system came crumbling down. Islamism, by contrast, is fueled by resentment, grievance, and more than a bit of envy, sentiments that often grow stronger the more that aggrieved Muslims see secondhand images of the West through the distortions of local media and the export of U.S. television programs that portray atypical slices of American society (e.g., *Dallas*, *Friends*). And though Islamism, as an ideology, is less than a century old, it draws on sources from more than a millennium ago and has far deeper roots in many societies than communism ever had.

In an operational sense, perhaps the most important contrast with the Cold War analogy is the need to be discriminating in promoting change in the Middle East. In the Cold War, engineering the demise of the Soviet Union and regime change within all Communist Bloc states was for many a cherished goal, even if not always a realistic short-term objective. In contrast, in the Middle East the objective is (with a few exceptions) reform, not regime change. However autocratic, stifling, illiberal, and, therefore, jihadist-producing the Egyptian, Tunisian, or Saudi regimes may be, the strategy to defeat Islamism must be rooted in promoting the sort of political, social, and economic change within existing regimes that denies Islamists opportunities for growth, not in creating a reign of political chaos from which Islamists, often a country's most powerful and best-organized political force, stand to benefit most.

Once again, the complexity of the task collides with its enormity. Take, for example, the promotion of democracy. There is no doubt that the development of truly representative, liberal, democratic political systems in Arab and Muslims states would be in the best interests of both the peoples of those countries and the West, just as it has been the case in Eastern Europe. However, there is no necessary reason to believe that Arab and Muslim countries would follow the same path as Eastern European states did, transitioning in little more than a decade from failed communist regimes into reasonably well-functioning democracies marching proudly into the European Union. Without careful and determined focus on the essential elements of democratic societies—promoting respect for basic freedoms and liberal ideals, strengthening the rule of law and its institutions—some Arab and Muslim countries could, under the banner of democracy, pivot into religiously inspired despotism that would make their current authoritarianism seem mild. At the same time, without a continual injection of urgency, a process of incremental liberalization can ossify and go sterile, especially if hijacked by reform-sounding reactionaries in the name of stability. And, along the way, the United States must keep its focus on the practical task of supporting democrats, those people who carry the daily burden of confronting the Islamists, not just the inspiring but often vague job of building democracy. This means extending a continual helping hand to America's natural allies—the hardy but often lonely band of Arab and Muslim liberals.

Here, finding the proper balance between incrementalism and comprehensiveness—between urgency and patience—is a major challenge. Move too slowly and the Islamists gain, while outside engines of reform lose legitimacy as they increasingly are viewed as defenders of an illegitimate status quo. Move too quickly and brittle regimes may either crack (offering a providential opening to Islamists) or fight back (in the process quashing any progress toward liberal reform), in either case undermining the larger effort. Finding the proper balance requires rhetoric that is as noble and inspirational as it is practical and direct. And it requires policies and programs that are designed to promote revolutionary change in an evolutionary fashion. This is, in effect, a strategy of "making haste, slowly." It will over time include different types of initiatives, incremental in speed, discriminate in place—all threads within the tapestry of fighting radical religious extremism through political, social, and economic reform.

To succeed, this strategy requires nimbleness, subtlety, and persistence. It needs to be informed by a healthy respect for the specifics of each country, but not such an overweening deference to local idiosyncrasies that it sidetracks the reform agenda. And it must be backed up by a heavy dose of political will that emanates from the hub and transmits, without slackening, to the end of all the spokes. In all these respects, the United States is, virtually by definition, ill suited to the task. But it nonetheless bears the lion's share of the burden for it, at least insofar as it is the principal agent of external dynamism in this process.

A Role for Private Initiatives

In promoting reform in the Middle East—as part of a larger strategy to make local governments more legitimate in the eyes of their citizenry, to deny Islamists fertile ground for growth, and, eventually, to drain the swamp in which they operate—Washington has a unique role to play. While any government can issue official reports on human rights violations, shower diplomatic attention on political reformers, engage local regimes in discussions over constitutional, legal, and administrative reform, praise or criticize the legitimacy of elections, and perform numerous other tasks, the U.S. government's posture on all these matters has special standing. The reach and effect of what private individuals, foundations, and organizations attempt to do in this context pales in comparison to that of the U.S. government.

Still, in terms of active efforts to promote reform in the Middle East, U.S. governmental initiatives are embryonic. The Bush administration's Middle East Partnership Initiative (MEPI) has sought to bridge the gap between traditional development aid and more politically oriented programming in the Middle East by focusing on four pillars: politics, economics, education, and women, with a special emphasis on youth. MEPI is based on the assumption that progress in these areas is a precondition for eventual political reform and democratization. According to its mission statement, MEPI endeavors, through numerous programs across the Middle East, to build synergies between private-sector, nongovernmental, international, and bilateral development initiatives.[3] While many of the programs it supports are promising and important, it is too early to tell whether MEPI has achieved success in its overseas operations or if it even has bureaucratic staying power inside the U.S. government.

Even newer to the field are plans to translate the Bush administration's expansive vision of a "forward strategy of freedom"[4] for Arabs and Muslims into a coherent Broader Middle East and North Africa Initiative working in tandem with European and Middle Eastern partners. Despite the decisions in this regard taken at the June 2004 G-8 summit at Sea Island, Georgia, the initiative is likely to remain a work in progress for a considerable time.[5]

Given this window, there is a greater opportunity for nongovernmental actors to play a role in promoting reform in the Middle East than would normally be the case. Private-sector initiatives deserve special consideration in this effort. While some nongovernmental organizations have been active in the Middle East for decades and will likely remain so, there are many other institutions—from the worlds of business, higher education, and philanthropy, for example—that have not focused their attention on the region. Initiatives by these private-sector actors could go far in complementing the still-early MEPI efforts in the region and infuse the overall reform agenda with energy and creativity.

In this regard, designers of private-sector initiatives to promote reform in Arab and Muslim societies should consider lifting a page from the Islamists' own operating manual: the power of example. Just as Islamist terrorists turn U.S. and Western advantages in size and power upside down by engineering asymmetric attacks against civilians, so too do Islamists operating in the civilian sector gain publicity, support, and perhaps even recruits through high-profile but relatively marginal asymmetric investments in social-welfare initiatives. Private-sector initiatives can operate on the same premise, whether financed and implemented by U.S. and Western nongovernmental organizations; universities; business, religious, or professional consortia; or groups of concerned individuals. They will never have the ability (i.e., the funds, the reach, or the personnel) to be agents of full-scale reform within Arab and Muslim societies, but that should not be their objective. A more limited, realistic, but still vitally important role for private-sector initiatives is to provide Western-oriented models of excellence as alternatives to the Islamist exemplars of reform. On that level, private-sector initiatives can make a major contribution to the reform dynamic.

A useful place for private-sector initiatives to begin is within three realms of action: media, education, and women. Obviously, these are not always clearly distinct groupings, as single programs can often target multiple objectives.

What follows is a menu of projects appropriate for private-sector initiatives in Arab and Muslim countries. It represents ideas drawn in part from an intensive set of group interviews held in autumn 2003 with intellectuals, journalists, businesspeople, and political figures from seven different Arab countries. It also represents the distillation of extensive contacts, conversations, and communications with interested parties in numerous Arab and Muslim countries. While pursuing these projects in coordination with U.S. government agencies (e.g., the State Department's MEPI office, the U.S. Agency for International Development, the Department of Commerce, the Department of Education) and local U.S. embassies would be beneficial, all can be undertaken independently of the U.S. government.

Media Initiatives

The past decade has seen fundamental change in the Arab media market. While commercial Arabic satellite television has been the most important new ingredient, the Arab media has also witnessed new and different types of newspapers, magazines, and nationally based television programming. Added to this is, of course, the introduction of the internet as a source of news for an elite, though growing, segment of society. Quality, however, has not kept pace with quantity. Despite notable pockets of professional journalism and reputable business practices, the Arab media industry suffers from sensationalist, ideological, often tendentious and fact-challenged journalism that is too frequently for sale to the highest bidder. Though not solely responsible for shaping Arab public opinion, it nevertheless is a major factor. No effort to promote liberal reform in Arab countries can succeed without some progress toward improving the quality of the media in these countries. Private-sector initiatives in the media industry can concentrate on three key areas:

1. Invest in upgrading professional standards of journalism in Arab and Muslim countries. Potential initiatives could include the following:

- Creating and expanding internship programs for local journalists at U.S. media outlets.

- Establishing specialized programs at U.S. journalism schools, especially for midcareer editors, journalists, and producers.

- Developing the use of distance-learning technology to link U.S. journalism schools with the many schools of communication around the Middle East. This could be a first step toward creating a full-fledged, American-style, English-language journalism school in the Middle East.

- Establishing, perhaps through the local American-style universities that currently exist in no fewer than five Arab countries, financial prizes for Arab journalists who report accurately and dispassionately on the United States—a local equivalent of the Polk Awards for foreign reporting.

- Supporting the establishment of a round-the-clock Arab media-watchdog operation—an Arab-based, Arab-staffed organization that professionally and dispassionately monitors the total content of Arab satellite and print media. Existing monitoring efforts, like the Middle East Media Research Institute (MEMRI), are extremely valuable but not comprehensive; in the eyes of many Arabs, they lack legitimacy because they are viewed as "cherry-picking" the most outrageous articles rather than reflecting the totality of Arab media coverage. (The accuracy of this charge is a separate issue.) Arab media lack, for example, the local equivalent of the Vanderbilt

University television news archive, which houses videotape of all television news broadcast in the United States, for scholarly and professional use.

2. Invest in alternative media. Potential initiatives could include supporting aspiring local media reformers. While the new, U.S. government–funded Arabic-language radio (Sawa) and television (al-Hurra) stations have attracted considerable attention—and sucked much of the oxygen from efforts to promote moderate, liberal alternatives to existing media outlets—there is still room for independent initiatives. In Morocco, for example, a group of dedicated liberals with considerable media experience is in search of financial backers for an educational satellite television station, currently dubbed "al-Moufida" (or "Useful TV"). Because this initiative and others like it across the region are based on local costs and expenses, budgets are a relative pittance.

3. Improve local media through the business side of the industry. Potential initiatives could include using advertising as a tool to leverage improvements in the Arab media. One of the great untold stories behind the sad state of the Arab media is the power of advertising dollars to control media content and the rampant corruption in the Arab advertising industry. Since U.S. corporations, operating through Middle East subsidiaries and local partners, play a considerable role in media advertising in the region, Americans have some leverage on this issue. Specifically, concerned citizens, perhaps acting in their capacity as corporate stockholders, can engage major U.S. corporations as well as the Advertising Council (the public interest arm of the advertising industry), demanding strict accountability for their advertising dollar and moderate, responsible content in the television programming and print outlets they patronize.

Educational Initiatives

Investing in education may not be the quickest route to political reform in Arab and Muslim countries, but without it such change is unlikely to occur and almost certainly will never take root. The problems facing education systems in many Middle Eastern countries are enormous, in terms of poorly trained, poorly paid, and poorly motivated teachers, inadequate physical plant, vast distances to schools without transportation, and an abject lack of educational materials. The demographic challenge that countries face in providing worthwhile[6] educational opportunities to millions of young people, so that they have useful life and employment skills by the time they leave school, is staggering. In this environment, the most that private-sector initiatives can do is target very specific, very narrow areas of problem and opportunity. The good news is that, in the education sector, even such specific, narrow projects touch real lives with lifelong impact. Perhaps more than in any other arena, the demonstration effect of successful private-sector initiatives is powerful and compelling. Some options for educational reform include the following:

1. Support models of excellence for students of all ages. The objective here is to underscore alternatives to failed government schools or madrasa-style rote education that too often traps students within an Islamist educational milieu at a young age.[7] Potential initiatives could include the following:

- Working with local communities and nongovernmental organizations (NGOs) to expand opportunities for "Head Start" type educational programs for young children. A derivative benefit is that such programs would provide a greater chance of employment for women, both in schools and during school hours.

- Investing in the creation, staffing, and physical plant of model schools (especially schools of science and technology) in major metropolitan areas. If starting from scratch, this should be done in tandem with local investors.

- Working with U.S. Chambers of Commerce and local U.S. corporations to fund or support work-study programs that mentor students through high school and provide guaranteed employment after graduation.

- Working with U.S. Chambers of Commerce and local investors to promote vocational training opportunities, the key missing link in the education chain in many Arab and Muslim countries.

2. Provide books and educational materials. Schools, universities, libraries, and private homes all suffer from a lack of books—of all kinds and for all ages—due to a range of factors: cost; the backward state of Arabic translation, publishing, and distribution networks; the low priority accorded to such nonrecurrent expenditures in government budgets; and the sheer overwhelming need for school supplies and educational materials in countries where demography creates massive spikes in the number of school-age children. Private-sector projects can make a dent in this problem through a variety of means:

- Contributing (financially or in kind) educational supplies to local schools and/or community libraries. This can be done through contact with local parent-teacher organizations or NGOs that operate in the education sector.

- Funding of collaborative programs with U.S.-based or even local American schools, which can "adopt" local Arab or Muslim schools and provide the latter with surplus educational materials as well as the human connection that comes with sister-school initiatives.

A logical activity for private-sector initiatives aimed at providing books and school supplies is supporting translation projects, perhaps in tandem with American-style universities in the Middle East, and subsidizing the publishing, marketing, and distribution of translated books. This is, in fact, a much more complicated, costly, and difficult undertaking than it seems at first glance.[8] Other than the idiosyncratic work of individual professors, the only independent nongovernmental institution involved in translating books into Arabic is the Beirut-based Arab Translation Organization (ATO), a low-budget, slow-paced operation. So far, fewer than a quarter of its forty-three planned books have been translated, and published, from the range of European languages. Initial print runs for each book have been only 2,000 copies, and ATO has never had cause (or resources) to produce second printings.

Outsiders attempting to enter the Arab book-translation market will find it to be an exceptionally murky business. Basic data on the state of the industry is hard to come by, which itself should send off warning signals to aspiring financiers of book translation. Moreover, by definition Arabic book translation violates one of the basic principles set out above: eschewing projects that rely on regional rather than national categorizations. Book translation and distribution has to be viewed in a regional context, but proceeding down that road exponentially increases the number of governmental and extragovernmental hurdles for any would-be private-sector initiative.

3. Invest in English-language education for all ages. Knowledge of English is the pathway to accessing American culture, society, and politics without the filter of local media, as well as the most efficient access route to the information highway. For Americans committed to promoting political reform through education, expanding opportunities for English-language education should be a top priority. Avenues through which to do so include the following:

- Supporting U.S. government–certified, English-language, American primary and secondary schools abroad, especially by establishing scholarship programs for students of modest means. These schools—approximately fifty of which already exist throughout Arab and Muslim countries—already provide top-quality, U.S.-style education to thousands of local students, mostly from wealthy elite families. Much more could be done to expand opportunities beyond that narrow circle.

- Supporting U.S. NGOs that take advantage of U.S. tax laws to collect, ship, and distribute American textbooks to schools, colleges, universities, and libraries abroad, working in tandem with local educational authorities or private charities.

- Supporting existing efforts, both nonprofit and commercial, to lower the cost of adult English-language education. Throughout the Middle East, there remains a vast untapped market for English instruction. Individual Americans should not be shy about seeking partnerships with local entrepreneurs to set up English-language training facilities.

Initiatives for Women

Focusing on women's role in public life should be a top priority for private-sector initiatives, with a special emphasis on education, legal reform, business, and the liberal professions. This is perhaps the most sensitive issue in Muslim societies, but, as eminent historian Bernard Lewis noted, it is the key battleground in the fight against Islamism:

> The emancipation of women, more than any other single issue, is the touchstone of difference between modernization and Westernization. . . . Both for traditional conservatives and radical fundamentalists it is neither necessary nor

useful but noxious, a betrayal of true Islamic values. It must be kept from entering the body of Islam, and where it has already entered, it must be ruthlessly excised.[9]

If reformers win the fight over women having both the opportunity (legal rights) and resources (education, employment) to play a role in all aspects of public life, then Islamists suffer a grievous blow; if reformers lose that fight, Islamists score a tremendous victory.

U.S. private initiatives are perhaps best suited to supporting efforts on two key fronts:

1. Helping local groups and organizations committed to advancing women's rights and opportunities. Potential initiatives could include the following:

- Supporting NGOs that provide shelters for abused women. (For example, a U.S. government program already supports such shelters in Jordan.)

- Supporting women's legal aid programs. While women have considerable rights on paper in many Arab and Muslim countries (e.g., concerning property, divorce, child custody), they often lack the education or means to ensure these rights are respected in court and before administrative authorities.

- Supporting women's collectives and cooperatives. Such initiatives need not be restricted to charity; business enterprises can also benefit from expertise in production, marketing, and distribution. These projects, which can provide much-needed employment opportunities for women, are particularly important given the high percentage of women (often with children) effectively abandoned by husbands who have sought their own employment opportunities in big cities or in Europe.

2. Focusing on girls' education, an area that clearly connects the larger emphases on women and education. Throughout the Middle East, illiteracy is a huge challenge; in many countries, illiteracy rates for women top 60 percent. As with the suggestions above, the role for private-sector initiatives is to highlight by example the commitment of Americans to improving this sorry situation. Efforts could include:

- Working with local or international NGOs to incentivize girls' education. One of the major impediments to girls' education is the fact that so many girls perform work that parents deem essential. Incentive-based initiatives effectively pay parents—perhaps by providing them with a mule, a cow, a plow, or some other practical assistance—to permit their daughters to attend school.

- Creating model academies for girls. Along the lines of model schools in metropolitan areas, these would be all-girl schools where parents can feel safe and confident about the environment of their daughters' education.

- Supporting projects to upgrade existing schools to make them "girl-friendly." Another impediment to girls' education is that parents often refuse to send their daughters to schools that lack adequate bathroom and other facilities that ensure privacy, hygiene, and decorum.

- Creating girl-focused mentoring programs with female professionals in all fields so that young and teenage girls have a firsthand understanding of alternative livelihoods, presented in culturally nonthreatening ways.

- Establishing via U.S. Chambers of Commerce special scholarships and mentoring programs that assist girls through high school and promise postgraduation employment. A special focus should be on girls' technical education.

After the What: How Many? Where? How?

Developing a useful formula for pursuing private-sector initiatives in the Middle East requires a mix of realism, idealism, persistence, expertise, and management skills that is difficult to create and even harder to sustain. On the one hand, private-sector activists need to be modest about the impact their efforts will have on the overall mission of political reform in Arab and Muslim countries. On the other hand, they still need to be bold enough to recognize that creating exemplars of an alternative future—for women, for students, for consumers of media—has the power to inspire and hence to change lives. The success of each initiative, therefore, is far more important than the actual number of initiatives. This is not a saturation strategy: it is a strategy of commitment.

Commitment also requires continuous supervision of all projects. The success or failure of many development projects is not measured in the start-up phase but in their ongoing operation. Many projects blossom in the early stages but lack the wherewithal—stamina among the original financiers, professionalism within the staff, ongoing interest of local partners, and continuing benefits to local citizenry—to persist over the medium and long term. It is essential that those motivated to pursue private-sector initiatives seek out experienced professionals to design and implement programs and be prepared to invest energy into consistent supervision of those programs over time.

Geographically, private-sector activists should be opportunistic. They should pursue openings where local governments, communities, and NGOs welcome outside initiatives and are receptive to foreign donors. Morocco, Jordan, Tunisia, and Yemen are natural candidates. (At times, working around local governments may, of course, be necessary.) These four countries have all been victims of Islamist terrorism; all are supportive, to varying degrees, of international efforts to combat it; all are engaged in efforts at political, social, and economic reform; and all have long histories of working with international aid agencies. Although the two major Arab media capitals, Cairo and Beirut, lie outside these four countries, that is more of an advantage than a disadvantage, as it provides a somewhat greater possibility that private-sector initiatives will get their start before scurrilous press coverage begins. Eventually, that will happen anyway, as even the least objectionable project in the most remote corner will be targeted by some newspaper or another. This is merely part of the price of doing business in many Arab and Muslim countries. Certain ideas outlined above—such as working with American schools abroad or with American-style English language universities—necessarily reach into other countries besides the four just mentioned. The key is to be discerning in choosing where to invest energies, funds, and commitment.

Lastly, private-sector activists must be willing to accept local partners as equals in all aspects of decisionmaking; to open their hearts, minds, and wallets to new ideas; and to forgo recognition for their benevolence. This is not to suggest that private initiatives should be giveaways. To the contrary, for many projects the likelihood of success will increase as more local financial partners can be identified to link up with outside donors. Despite vast poverty in many Arab and Muslim countries, there is also considerable wealth that should be tapped to help realize many of the ideas described above.[10]

All in all, successful private initiatives will be those animated exclusively by the mission of assisting Arabs and Muslims to counter the spread of Islamism by advancing down the path of reform, liberalism, and democracy. Adding other agendas into the mix is a recipe for failure.

Notes

1. Both President George W. Bush and Senator John Kerry have made appeals for sustained engagement with allies and Arab and Muslim friends to promote political reform, democracy, and human rights throughout the Greater Middle East.

2. See, for example, the signal speech in this regard by German foreign minister Joschka Fischer at the Fortieth Munich Conference on Security Policy, February 7, 2004.

3. For details, see the Middle East Partnership Initiative website (http://mepi.state.gov/mepi).

4. See President Bush's speeches on the subject at Whitehall Palace in London (November 19, 2003; available online at www.whitehouse.gov/news/releases/2003/11/20031119-1.html), before the American Enterprise Institute (February 26, 2003; available online at www.whitehouse.gov/news/releases/2003/02/20030226-11.html), and at the National Endowment for Democracy (November 6, 2003; available online at www.whitehouse.gov/news/releases/2003/11/20031106-2.html).

5. For more information on the Sea Island initiatives, see White House Office of the Press Secretary, "Fact Sheet: Broader Middle East and North Africa Initiative," June 9, 2004. Available online (www.state.gov/e/eb/rls/fs/33380.htm).

6. "Worthwhile" is a key word here. Whereas the focus of education reform in the past was to increase student enrollment, this was often done without adequate regard to the content of education that students received in schools. This led to a situation in which some governments were able to claim huge achievements in student enrollments, while millions of students still left school without the skills—including literacy—necessary to function in society.

7. It would be a mistake, both of tactics and of morals, for advocates of reform to fight against Muslim religious education per se. Islam is a source of inspiration to more than a billion people, and Muslim parents are justifiably proud of children who learn about religious history, teachings, and text through religious education. The key point to underscore is the need for choice: parents should not be forced to send their children to religious schools as the only educational alternative for their children.

8. The most widely quoted data on book translation into Arabic comes from the UN Development Program's 2003 Arab Human Development Report (AHDR), which relied heavily on the research of an Egyptian, Shawki Galal. A researcher for this essay, Martin Schneider, contacted Galal and, over the course of several conversations, reached the conclusion that Galal's information was as much the product of informed speculation as it was provable research. For example, Galal asserted that about 350 books per year are translated into Arabic (the source of the much-quoted AHDR statistic that "Five times more books are translated yearly into Greek, a language spoken by just 11 million people, than into Arabic.") When pressed for a list of recent translations, however, Galal could produce only eighty titles, suggesting that the Arabic translation industry is even worse off than commonly thought.

9. Bernard Lewis, *What Went Wrong: Western Impact and Middle Eastern Response* (New York: Oxford, 2002), p. 73.

10. "Challenge grants" are particularly appropriate, for example, in creating scholarships at U.S. schools and improving the physical plant of local schools to encourage girls' attendance. For more commercial ideas, such as establishing science and math academies or English-language training centers for adults, finding local partners is essential.

Lessons from the Front Line:
My Two Years in Morocco

August 2004

MOROCCO IS A NATION OF NEARLY 30 MILLION PEOPLE, part Arab, part Berber, and overwhelmingly Muslim, yet distant enough from Iraq and the Israeli-Palestinian arena so that those issues, while relevant, are not all-consuming. Hence, it provides an excellent vantage point from which to assess the ideological battle between radical Islamists, on the one hand, and non- and anti-Islamists on the other.

Like many countries in the region, Morocco has been passing through turbulent times. It is on the front line in the war on terrorism, as evidenced by the May 16, 2003, suicide bombings in Casablanca and many other failed plots that have gone unreported. Wahhabi institutions are widespread, especially in the north, and Moroccans have played key roles in numerous al-Qaeda conspiracies. As elsewhere, however, the daily lives of ordinary Moroccans are not consumed by this overarching reality.

My own case was unusual: in March 2003, nearly halfway through my two-year stay in Morocco, I was the target of a front-page attack in *at-Tajdid*, the newspaper of the country's radical Islamist movement. This was followed by an attack in the influential leftist newspaper, *Le Journal*. In a small way, then, I joined the ideological battle facing the larger Moroccan society. This is a real-life battle for the hearts, minds, and pocketbooks of millions of people in dozens of countries: from parents eager to secure the finest possible education for their children only to learn that the schools with the best facilities and highest-paid teachers are privately financed Islamist academies, to small businessmen turned down by banks for loans and forced to turn to Islamist loan sharks, who extract a political price in lieu of interest.

Originally published as *PolicyWatch* number 889, August 2, 2004.

During my first year in Morocco, the Islamists were in ascendance. They had compelled the king, Muhammad VI, to shelve proposals for reform of the family code and had effectively won a nationwide parliamentary election. In May 2003, however, everything changed. The coordinated terrorist attacks in Casablanca—most of which targeted Jewish sites—provoked widespread popular revulsion. After three weeks of silence, the regime finally acted; its courageous and assertive new approach was worth the wait. It included strong rhetoric (e.g., condemnations of radical ideas from "the east," a thinly veiled reference to Wahhabism), aggressive security measures (e.g., a new antiterrorism law), official ostracization of Islamist political parties (who received just 3 percent of the vote in subsequent nationwide municipal elections), ideological countermeasures (e.g., increased control over mosques and vetting of sermons), bold reform measures (e.g., sweeping change of the family code, ending legal discrimination against women), and even increased openness regarding Arab-Israeli matters (e.g., a public welcome for Israel's foreign minister).

Collectively, these initiatives constituted a major change in both substance and style. They were made possible by two factors: leadership and receptivity. First, Morocco had a leader who decided to get serious about the range of problems facing his country. Second, it had a populace that was, by and large, disgusted by terrorist violence and had become willing to accept change.

Morocco has also continued to progress on democratization by enhancing elections, decentralization, and other key processes. Although it is still a country in which the monarch both reigns and rules, it is moving in the right direction. A case in point was the messy but fundamentally healthy political give-and-take between officials in Rabat and elected local representatives regarding disbursal of relief aid following the February 24, 2004, earthquake in al-Hoceima.

At the same time, it is essential to recognize the inherent tension between democratization and the fight against extremism. Democracy promotion and the hearts-and-minds campaign are first cousins, not identical twins. Democratization is about creating rules, institutions, and patterns of behavior in which local people can determine their own future, peacefully, over time. The battle for hearts and minds is about empowering local people to defeat the creeping totalitarianism of radical Islamists. Without victory in the latter struggle, the former stands no chance.

To win this battle, the U.S. government needs to reconsider the nature of the problem. As the 9-11 Commission argued, the problem is not terrorism, it is the ideology from which terrorists spring, i.e., radical Islamism. The appropriate strategic response is for the United States to be firm and clear in its values. Tactically, Washington needs to use every arrow in its quiver, from diplomacy (both public and traditional) to military power.

The United States must also rethink its understanding of the protagonists in this struggle. What, for example, is a "Moroccan"? Many are Arabs, but at least half are Berber. Many speak Arabic as their first language, but many others do not. This demographic kaleidoscope is actually the norm in what is erroneously called "the Arab world," many parts of which are home to large percentages of non-Arabs and non-Sunnis. Translating this reality into rhetoric and policy is essential.

Moreover, this reality reaches beyond demographics to politics. In Morocco, for example, most Arabic speakers plead not to be lumped in with Arabs from mashrek, or the "east"—i.e., those Arabs who are hung up on Israel, seduced by Wahhabism, or party to other crazy ideologies like Baathism. This is not to suggest that Iraq and the Israeli-Palestinian conflict are not important and emotive issues in Morocco. Their urgency and relevance waxes and wanes with time, however. Sentiments expressed by Moroccans (and others) on these issues, while real, should not be exaggerated. Assessing the operational relevance of these sentiments is key.

In this regard, public opinion polls that suggest near-universal hatred of the United States in the Arab and Muslim worlds must be viewed with extreme caution. Not only is the methodology sometimes faulty, but positive responses to questions about the United States are rarely highlighted, while negative responses are underscored. For example, the Pew Global Attitudes Project's March 2004 report was titled *A Year After the Gulf War: Mistrust of America in Europe Ever Higher, Muslim Anger Persists*. Yet, one would search the report in vain for any polling question that actually asked Muslims about levels of anti-U.S. "anger."

The spread of radical Islamism, not U.S. unpopularity, is the most serious challenge to U.S. interests in many Arab and Muslim societies. The solution—as frequently expressed by liberal Moroccans—cannot be found in reaching an accommodation with the Islamists. Such a policy sends a doubly bad message. First, it tells the Islamists that they are powerful enough to goad Washington into overlooking their rejection of virtually every American value in order to build a relationship with them. Second, it tells non- and anti-Islamists that they are not important enough to merit America's attention. Specifically, anti-Islamist Moroccans complain that Washington sends the wrong message when it provides parliamentary training funds that are used by Islamist legislators to become more effective critics of the government; when it pays to send Islamists to the inaugural Congress of Muslim Democrats, giving them a U.S. stamp of approval; and when, as reported in the Moroccan press, it advises the regime against banning the legal Islamist party, the Party of Justice and Development, following the May 2003 bombings.

Based on my experience in Morocco, U.S. public diplomacy needs to focus on three key areas: image, interests, and investments. Regarding the first element, America's image matters, and there are many steps—often commonsensical—that could be taken to improve it (e.g., having diplomats speak local languages). But image is about the present; Washington needs to think much more about the future. Hence, focusing on interests and investments is essential.

In advancing its interests, the U.S. government should begin by taking Arabs and Muslims more seriously. In particular, Washington must abandon its longstanding reluctance to talk directly to Arab and Muslim audiences about difficult issues such as terrorism, radical Islamism, the Arab-Israeli conflict, and Iraq.

Unfortunately, the most important element in U.S. public diplomacy—the need to invest in both current allies and the potential for future ones—is the least valued. This effort should have three components:

- **Identify allies.** Unlike Islamists, non- and anti-Islamist Muslims are defined more by who they are not rather than by who they are. They range across political tendencies and include all types of Muslims, from radical atheists to lapsed Muslims to pious believers. The U.S. role should be to identify potential allies among these individuals and build networks of common purpose among them. Just as the United States forged an anti-Nazi alliance with communists during World War II, the anti-Islamist effort may involve bringing together people of very different worldviews to work collectively toward the larger cause. Washington also needs to show these individuals that it is willing to support them in the currency that matters, i.e., visibility and money. Contrary to popular opinion, the imprimatur of the United States remains sorely coveted, especially in terms of money. As virtually all U.S. Agency for International Development or embassy officials report across the Middle East, very few local nongovernmental organizations (NGOs) have actually rejected offers of U.S. financial aid in protest of U.S. policy.

- **Empower allies.** The U.S. government needs to strengthen its local anti-Islamist allies. One important means of doing so is to provide them with the information necessary to fight the Islamists. For example, anti-Islamists share a growing alarm at the spread of Islamist social-welfare activities, some of which are linked to terrorist front groups. Many civic activists, including journalists, would take up the cudgel against these groups, especially if they knew about their possible terrorist connections. They lack such information, however, even though much of it is available in the public record in the United States. One solution would be the creation of an internet-based information clearinghouse in Arabic and other local languages, outlining the operations, management, financing, and personnel of all Islamist-oriented initiatives and NGOs and the linkages between them.

- **Nurture future allies.** The United States needs to invest time, effort, and money in developing new and future allies. For Islamists, education—especially children's education—is the prime battleground. So far, the United States is barely even putting up a fight.

Promoting English-language education should be America's top priority. While knowing English does not necessarily translate into liberal thought or pro-American sentiment, English is a portal to both Anglo-American culture and the internet-based information revolution. Knowing English at least gives someone the opportunity to learn about the United States and make judgments about its policies and values without the filter of translation or reliance on sources of information that may present a skewed image of reality. Specific initiatives that could be pursued include:

- Creating "English-for-all" after-school programs throughout the Muslim world at no or nominal cost to parents. This could be pursued cooperatively with existing NGOs and the governments of other English-speaking countries. Few steps could earn the United States more goodwill in Muslim countries than investing enough money to make English-language study free or very low in cost.

- Supporting the development of U.S.-style, English-language universities, with the goal of having at least one fully-accredited English-language university in every country in the Middle East.

- Expanding the paltry financial support for American schools abroad to provide American-style educational opportunities for school-age children. In an age when embassies are fortresses, American schools (and the Peace Corps) are the only open and welcoming institutions of Americana left in many countries. They deserve more help. One idea, born of my own family's experience, is the American School Abroad Support Act (HR 4303), which would provide full or partial merit-based scholarships for lower- and middle-class Arab and Muslim children to attend certified American schools overseas.

The bottom line is, the United States need not be defeatist. There are millions of Muslims who are not only willing to fight against radical Islamists, but are already engaged in fighting them on a daily basis in their own communities. The United States needs to make common cause with these brave individuals, providing support so that they can fight their battle more effectively. Their battle is America's—and their victory will be America's victory, too.

Polls Apart: Why Public Opinion Surveys Should Not Define Public Diplomacy

September 2004

C HANCES ARE THAT YOU HAVE NEVER READ THIS PARA-graph in your morning newspaper:

> In startling poll results released today, Muslims around the world overwhelmingly endorsed America's role as the world's lone super-power, with huge majorities saying that international security would be endangered by the emergence of a global competitor to the United States.

And you probably have never heard a TV anchor announce this item on a network news show:

> Confounding news reports of a deepening sense of crisis throughout the Muslim world, poll results released today show that Muslims around the globe are gener-ally satisfied with the way things are going inside their countries. By contrast, citizens of every Western country polled— including the United States—say they are increasingly unhappy with the direction of their own countries.

And you almost surely have never flipped through a glossy newsmagazine to find this tidbit:

> One year after the Iraq war sent thousands of Middle Easterners into the streets to protest the U.S.-led invasion, Arabs increasingly give the United States a passing grade for its performance in Iraq, according to the results of a highly respected international public opinion survey released today.

All of these conclusions are drawn from the raw data of a nine-nation survey conducted in February–March 2004 by the Pew Foundation's Global Atti-tudes Project.[1] Yet when the foundation released the poll results on March

Previously unpublished essay.

16, 2004, under the title *A Year after Iraq War: Mistrust of America in Europe Ever Higher, Muslim Anger Persists*, none of these findings were included in the press package or the accompanying analytical report.[2] Instead the Pew press advisory highlighted survey results that only showed a deepening divide between the United States and Arab and Muslim peoples. This prompted Cassandra-like headlines in newspapers across the country, such as "Poll Finds Hostility Hardening toward U.S. Policies" (*New York Times*), "Opinion of U.S. Abroad is Falling, Survey Finds" (*Washington Post*), and "Polls Show Surge in Anti-U.S. Views" (*Chicago Tribune*).

The "Pew polls," as they are widely known, are generally recognized as the gold standard of international public opinion surveys; they are guided by a stellar advisory group of international statesmen and academic experts and employ some of the most advanced and progressive polling methods. Along with polls by Gallup, Zogby International, and other survey firms, the Pew project did indeed find deeply disturbing developments in Arab and Muslim attitudes toward the United States. From respondents' sympathies with Osama bin Laden to their views of the legitimacy of the U.S.-led "war on terror," the picture that emerged was bleak.

But the polls did not, in fact, paint as bleak a picture as the pollsters claimed they did. In reporting the poll findings, Pew not only downplayed any reference to good news about Arab and Muslim attitudes, but its pollsters also seem to have massaged the analytical findings to make them appear even more hysterically anti-American than the numbers suggested.

Indeed, the very title of the poll report displayed a certain sleight of hand. Although it headlined the extent of "Muslim anger," nothing in the poll itself measured the level of "anger." In fact, the word "anger" does not even appear in the poll questionnaire. Muslims did give very high "unfavorable" ratings to the United States, but there is considerable difference between viewing something unfavorably and being angry with it.

If one takes the poll findings in their totality, the results were not all bleak—far from it. The poll surveyed four countries—Morocco, Jordan, Turkey, and Pakistan—whose collective population constitutes about one-sixth of the Muslim world. The picture that emerges from the poll's raw data is one of stunning contradiction, not a mind-numbing series of anti-American outbursts. Consider two counterintuitive results from Morocco:

- Conventional wisdom holds that Arabs hate U.S. government policies, not the American people. But in one of the most head-scratching findings in the Pew poll, the percentage of Moroccans who viewed Americans unfavorably grew by one-third between 2003 and 2004 while views of the United States itself were unchanged.

- By a large majority, Moroccans said that their experience since the Iraq war had given them less confidence that Washington truly wants to promote democracy around the world. But when asked whether they believe that the United States favors democracy in their country, Moroccans said "yes" by a margin of nearly two-to-one.

While the Pew pollsters highlighted the negative aspects of both sets of findings, they made virtually no mention of the positive aspects. If one takes account of all the data produced by a first-class survey like the Pew poll, then the picture that emerges of the Middle East is much more nuanced than the commonly held image of a region in which crazed anti-Americans (or, in some depictions, crazed Bush-haters) burn Uncle Sam in effigy in the streets of Arab capitals.

The reality, as usual, is more complex. Bouts of mass anti-Americanism are real, powerful but episodic. They are often as fleeting as the televised images of placard-waving Iraqi crowds or Israeli-Palestinian carnage, which themselves often trigger rounds of anti-Washington recrimination. Like many Americans, Arabs and Muslims are fully capable of holding conflicting views of the Bush administration—for example, welcoming its vocal promotion of democracy while deriding its perceived heavy-handedness in Iraq or its close friendship with Israel.

Moreover, it would be a mistake to think that the vast majority of the world's 1.3 billion Muslims spend their waking hours focusing on any of these political topics. For most, the daily priorities are finding good homes, good jobs, and good schools. For many, just eking out a living—food, shelter, basic healthcare—dominates the day. If any political issue predominates, it is not related to the United States, Israel, or Iraq, but rather concerns the bitter contest—underway in virtually every Muslim-majority country—between Islamists who wish to control social, cultural, and economic life as a stepping stone to political power, and the loose and leaderless network of non- and anti-Islamist Muslims who are fighting against them.

Perceptions do matter, however, and understanding public opinion therefore has a role to play in shaping U.S. policy. Since Islamists exploit the idiom of anti-Americanism to advance their cause, Washington needs to tailor its message more thoughtfully and creatively to Muslim audiences. Even so, the most useful alteration in the U.S. message would come with improving the moral and material assistance that Americans provide to Muslims who contend every day with the creeping struggle against extremism. A poll-centric approach, however, has the effect of transforming the difficult but doable task of helping these anti-Islamists into mission impossible. Islamist extremism may be their number-one enemy, but American defeatism could be a close second.

Israeli statesman Shimon Peres, a tireless campaigner who ran—and lost—numerous races for prime minister, once famously said that polls are like perfume: beautiful to smell, deadly to drink. While they can help inform our view of Arab and Muslim political thinking, they should not be allowed to define it. This is especially the case when pollsters appear to prefer the "shock and awe" method of portraying survey results rather than dispassionately presenting the full complexity of Arab and Muslim political behavior.

So, when you read the inevitable screaming headlines about the next Pew, Gallup, or Zogby poll in the Middle East, take them with a grain of salt. Although there are indeed dark clouds hovering above many Arab and Muslim countries, the sky is not falling. Every day, millions of Muslims—secular, lapsed, or pious—are fighting to prevent Islamist radicalism from taking control of their cities, towns, and villages. Whether they agree or disagree with Washington's troop deployment in Iraq or its support of Israel is much less important than whether they have our support in this life-and-death struggle.

Notes

1. Question 16 of the survey asked whether respondents "think the world would be a safer place or a more dangerous place if there was another country that was equal in power to the United States." According to the raw poll data, the number of respondents who feared the consequences of the emergence of a global competitor to the United States compared to those who did not were 65 percent to 21 percent in Morocco; 61 to 18 percent in Pakistan; 53 to 29 percent in Jordan; and 46 to 41 percent in Turkey. On whether respondents were satisfied or dissatisfied with the way things were going in their country in February–March 2004 as compared with May 2003 (question 1), the number of "satisfied" respondents increased from 34 percent to 58 percent in Morocco; from 42 to 59 percent in Jordan; from 29 to 54 percent in Pakistan; and from 19 to 40 percent in Turkey. On grading whether the United States and its allies were taking into account the needs and interests of the Iraqi people in rebuilding their country (question 20), the number of respondents

who replied "poor" (with the other options being "excellent," "good," and "only fair") in February–March 2004, compared to May 2003, dropped from 47 percent to 37 percent in Morocco, from 55 to 37 percent in Jordan, and from 43 to 34 percent in Pakistan. Only in Turkey did the percentage responding "poor" rise, a modest two-point increase (from 36 percent to 38 percent). The full text of the questionnaire with poll results is available online (http://people-press.org/reports/print.php3?PageID=798).

2. These and other materials related to the Pew poll are available online (http://people-press.org/reports/display.php3?ReportID=206).

The Battle of Ideas in the War on Terror: Fighting the Fight

September 2004

I N JANUARY 2005, THE NEXT PRESIDENT WILL FIND HIMSELF leading a nation fighting wars on five fronts at once. Four are clear: in Iraq and Afghanistan, against al-Qaeda and its global affiliates, and within the homeland. While Americans may vigorously debate how we find ourselves fighting on so many fronts at once, there is no substantial disagreement on the need to expend considerable blood and treasure to ensure victory (or at least prevent defeat) on all of them. Indeed, a common critique of the Bush administration is that it has not asked *enough* sacrifice from the citizenry—in the form of forgoing tax cuts, for example—at a time of such intense national peril.

The fifth front, however, is the poor stepsister to the other four. It is being fought with an arsenal of outmoded and dysfunctional weaponry, a set of confused and self-defeating battlefield tactics, and no clear strategy for victory. While the president himself may understand the stakes, his commanders routinely snipe at each other over such usual bureaucratic prizes as money and manpower. Even worse, in the heat of battle, they are still arguing over who are our enemies and who are our allies.

Such is the status of the U.S. effort to fight the "battle of ideas"—the ideological war to prevent radical Islamists from capturing the social, cultural, economic, and eventually political high ground in Muslim societies around the world.

Those who dismiss this contest as being a public relations challenge and not a potentially cataclysmic life-and-death struggle are wrong. The choice between Islamists and non- and anti-Islamists is not the same as the choice

Previously unpublished essay.

between Labor and Conservative in Britain or Ariel Sharon and Shimon Peres in Israel; it is far more akin to the choice between a communist and free society at the height of the Cold War. The Islamist alternative poses a form of totalitarian threat to societies, governments, and nations covering more than a billion people in dozens of countries; it is a challenge to values, policies, and interests, all at once. While this is principally a fight being waged by Muslims within each individual society, the United States cannot avoid its role as a central player; American values, policies, and interests are at stake as well. It is a series of national struggles within a global context, and a string of individual national defeats could spell a catastrophe for U.S. interests and ruin for America's friends on three continents.

Despite all this, the battle of ideas fights for the scraps left over from the four other fronts. Whereas the others have a privileged call on the full weight of American might, the ideological front suffers from the weakest bureaucratic champions, the least resources, and the fewest headlines. Despite the considerable good news that goes unreported even on this front—such as the growing recognition among Western leaders of the enormity of the threat as well as the proven determination of millions of non- and anti-Islamist Muslims to resist the expansion of radical Islamism—goodwill and commitment alone will not win the fight. If the United States is to play an effective role in helping Muslim allies win the societal battle against radical Islamists and in rallying Western nations to support that cause, fixing the conceptual faults and structural defects in U.S. policy must be one of the new president's first tasks.

The key lies in recognizing the urgency of the ideological challenge posed by radical Islamism, understanding the importance of winning this fight as prerequisite to the systemic political and social changes in Muslim societies that would benefit U.S. national security, and committing the human, material, and political resources to achieve it.

In this regard, President Bush has performed a vital service by drawing the link between the failures of Arab and Muslim societies and their impact on U.S. interests. In rhetoric, at least, he has changed two generations of U.S. foreign policy, by placing "democracy promotion" above "stability maintenance" as a strategic desideratum. Whether his and subsequent administrations operate on that premise, Bush's increasingly stirring speeches have had the effect of making political and social reform within Arab and Muslim countries an item of national security interest, not just humanitarian "do-gooder" concern.

But the administration's rhetorical flourishes—which have been important in putting Arab Muslim autocrats on notice about the potential for changed U.S. priorities, energizing millions of anti-Islamist Muslims, and laying down the gauntlet to ideological adversaries around the world—mask an intellectual fuzziness about the strategic objective of U.S. policy. In turn, that fuzziness has seeped into policy, leading to the creation of bureaucracies that compete against one another to promote contradictory and often self-defeating ways to advance the president's "forward strategy of freedom" in Arab and Muslim societies.

The basic problem is threefold: a lack of clarity, a lack of priorities, and a lack of urgency.

First, the lack of clarity is evident in the fact that so many offices and bureaus have a finger in this effort. Depending on who in the U.S. government is offering the definition of the problem, fighting the battle of ideas can include promoting economic and social development; strengthening human rights and the prospects for liberal democracy; and deepening knowledge of U.S. society, values, and interests. While textbook "public diplomacy" focuses on the last of those three goals, the essence of public diplomacy in the post–September 11 world must involve integrating all of these objectives at the right pace and with the proper dose. Yet each of those three missions has its own bureaucratic home—the U.S. Agency for International Development, the Undersecretariat of Public Diplomacy and Public Affairs in the Department of State, and the Bureau of Democracy, Labor, and Human Rights, a subsidiary element of the Public Diplomacy Undersecretariat—each of which is keen to advance its particular goals and ideological bent. In addition, the new Middle East Partnership Initiative (MEPI), housed in the Bureau of Near Eastern Affairs, has a mandate to promote innovative paths to "reform" that, in practice, touches on all these missions. And after September 11, the White House created two additional addresses—the Office of Global Communications, which was charged with coordinating strategic communications from the U.S. government to overseas audiences, and the Strategic Communication Policy Coordinating Committee (SCPCC), to ensure interagency coordination in public diplomacy.

The bureaucratic reality is that all have tended to encroach on the mandates of the others. When everyone has responsibility, the practical implication is that none do. Indeed, a scathing report by the General Accounting Office (GAO) released in August 2004 noted that the SCPCC—the body charged with integrating all governmental initiatives in public diplomacy toward Arab and Muslim societies—did not convene even once in the sixteen months following the U.S. invasion of Iraq.[1]

Second, the priorities problem is apparent from the lack of strategy that governs America's effort to wage the battle of ideas. The GAO report offered a damning critique: "There is still no interagency strategy to guide State's and all federal agencies communications efforts and ensure consistent messages to overseas audiences. In addition, as of June 2004, State still lacks a comprehensive and commonly understood public diplomacy strategy to guide its programs."[2] The absence of a well-conceived, intellectually honest strategy for advancing U.S. interests among Muslim peoples means that various arms of the government have license to promote their own individual strategies.

A case in point is the blurring of the distinction between public diplomacy and democracy promotion. They are not identical; at best, they are first cousins. Traditionally, public diplomacy is about developing understanding for U.S. policies, interests, and values abroad so as to build support for America among foreign peoples; democracy promotion is about empowering foreign peoples to develop free, independent, and representative governments so they can make decisions for themselves.

The fact is that the latter is wholly dependent on the former; only when societies are either free from the Islamist challenge or at least have found effective, ongoing means to control it can they then proceed safely down the path of liberalization, democratization, and eventual democracy. While advancing certain liberal ideals—such as free elections or women's equality—are worthy policy goals, in the heat of the battle of ideas they need to be viewed, first and foremost, as tools in the fight against the spread of radical Islamism.

A misreading of tactical priorities often produces ideas that are noble in intent but have the practical effect of undermining the larger strategic goal. Such, for example, is the case with many of the U.S.-funded programs designed to promote "institution building" in Arab and Muslim societies. These are, logically enough, designed to strengthen such worthy icons of a liberal society as parliaments, political parties, and the civil society sector, as well as basic freedoms such as speech, assembly, and redress. But focusing on the abstraction of the institution, rather than on the people who occupy that institution, can lead to the absurd situation of U.S. funding of radical Islamists—Islamist parliamentarians, Islamist educators, Islamist internet entrepreneurs, etc. In other words, our programming toward Arabs and Muslims should not be so fixated on form that it is blind to content. Some might view this as a reasonable price to pay to deepen the otherwise weak foundations of these institutions in many societies. That position, however, is usually not shared by America's non- and anti-Islamist Muslim allies who are frequently stunned to learn that their adversaries benefit from American largesse and political imprimatur, all in the name of liberal ideals.

Third, the lack of urgency is reflected in the meager political, human, and financial capital devoted to the task. Important things are worth paying for and there is little evidence that the battle of ideas rates highly on the list of post–September 11 national security priorities.

On the political level, the president articulated a fundamental shift in U.S. foreign policy—away from a cozy, sixty-year-old relationship with status quo regimes toward a new "forward strategy for freedom" in the Middle East—but it is difficult to discern who is in charge of making it happen. There is no National Security Council (NSC) directorate dedicated to this issue; while the White House was indeed consumed with Middle East reform proposals in the context of the June 2004 G-8 summit at Sea Island, Georgia, it evidently passed off responsibility for the Broader Middle East and North Africa Initiative to the State Department shortly after the event. And it was only in July 2004 that the successor to the SCPCC was established, under joint NSC-State chairmanship.

To the extent there is a single person responsible for all non-broadcasting aspects of the battle of ideas—the commander-in-chief for this theater of war—it is the undersecretary of state for public diplomacy. Since September 11, that position has been held by two different people, Charlotte Beers and Margaret Tutwiler. Although both are very accomplished professionals, neither had a particularly successful tenure in the post. This was due partly to the structure of the portfolio and partly to an analytical misreading of the challenges they faced and the tools needed to overcome them. What is most striking, however, is that political circumstances make it virtually impossible to have a successor in place before spring 2005; in the meantime, no one—neither a presidential advisor nor secretarial counselor—has been given this vital portfolio to supervise. In the midst of a Middle East war, could one imagine the U.S. military permitting the position of CENTCOM commander-in-chief to remain vacant for a week, let alone nine months? Clearly, this says something about the lack of urgency attached to the battle of ideas.

On the financial front, the story is similar. Apart from international broadcasting—which won favor from both the White House and Congress despite being the arm of public diplomacy least able to achieve a long-term impact—spending on public diplomacy in real dollars has decreased since September 11. (While many ill-conceived and poorly implemented programs deserve to have their budgets cut, many others—such as targeted exchange programs, educational projects, and English-language initiatives—merit a sizable infusion of extra cash.) It is true that MEPI did receive "new money" to promote its ambitious agenda of "reform." Coupled with management that is proving creative, innovative, and empowered to circumvent traditional bureaucratic barriers, MEPI is indeed one of the few post–September 11 bright spots in terms of U.S. public diplomacy. But one can hardly be sanguine about jump-starting too much "reform" via a series of regional projects and fourteen country-specific programs with the total of $129 million that has so far been appropriated.[3]

And as for human capital, so many reports have chronicled the shocking lack of language facility among U.S. diplomats in Arab and Muslim societies that the numbers no longer shock. Nevertheless, they bear repeating: According to the August 2004 GAO report, more than one-fifth of all "language-designated" positions around the world are filled with foreign service officers lacking required skills; the region with the highest percentage not meeting the requirements was the Middle East, with 30 percent; in South Asia, not one of eight "language-preferred" positions was filled with a language-proficient FSO.[4] While there are many reasons for this situation, the one that is most important is the apparent triviality of the entire issue. If the U.S. military sent soldiers into battle with shoddy training and obsolete weaponry, it would be a national scandal; regrettably, the "battle of ideas" merits neither the same investment nor similar scrutiny.

Given this depressing litany of problems with the U.S. government's public diplomacy effort in the Middle East, what can be done to repair the damage? Here are three suggestions:

- Though there are obvious differences, the battle of ideas should be viewed more like a military front—as with Iraq, Afghanistan, or the homeland—and less like one of many diplomatic initiatives. The goal, admittedly over the long term, should be victory, not just progress. It is the president's responsibility, through his national security advisor, to ensure that strategies and tactics are clearly defined; that lines of authority are streamlined throughout departments, bureaus, and agencies; and that sufficient resources (training, money, etc.) are provided to enable our diplomat-soldiers in the field to do their jobs. None of this will happen without breaking some bureaucratic china. In the near term, this may require the appointment of a senior presidential advisor with overall responsibility for directing and coordinating the disparate U.S. government public diplomacy initiatives, now spread among a wide array of bureaucracies.

- In its outreach abroad, the United States should attempt to do fewer things better. In the pre–September 11 era, America could afford to spend millions of dollars on projects and programs that had certain humanitarian, developmental, or cultural importance but which had, at most, a tangential impact on the battle of ideas. Today, however, we should target our resources more narrowly, with strategic objectives clearly in mind. For example, Washington should consider making educational reform—curricular reform, teacher training, schoolbook provision, new scholarships, English-language initiatives—the central focus of U.S. development efforts in Muslim societies, leaving the lead role in many traditional development areas (health, clean water, etc.) to other international aid donors.

- U.S. public diplomacy efforts must become more local, entrepreneurial, and aggressive. In every Muslim society, U.S. officials must actively seek out potential allies, develop future partners, and have the freedom to take risks with each. It is far better to gamble on assisting a local partner who claims to share an antipathy to radical Islamism and fail in the effort than to "cover one's bets" through a counterproductive attempt to reach a *modus vivendi* with the Islamists themselves.

Winning the battle of ideas will not be easy. But step one is to realize that it is a battle, and step two is to realize that it can be won. Even with clarity, priorities, and urgency, the next president—whether the reelected incumbent or his victorious challenger—may not be able to steer the United States and its allies to victory. But at least he can get us into the fight.

Notes

1. The GAO report noted that the State Department established a body called the Policy Coordinating Committee on the Muslim World Initiative, which effectively took over the role of the SCPCC. However, this was not until July 2004—sixteen months after the SCPCC was reported to have last met. See "U.S. Public Diplomacy: State Department and Broadcasting Board of Governors Expand Post-9/11 Efforts, But Challenges Remain," GAO-04-1061T, testimony of Jess T. Ford, director of GAO's Office of International Affairs and Trade, released on August 23, 2004, p. 10.

2. Ibid., p. 9.

3. As of September 4, 2004, the MEPI website (http://mepi.state.gov/mepi) reported that "to date, the administration has committed $129 million to MEPI ($29 million in FY 2002 supplemental and $100 million in FY 2003 supplemental)."

4. GAO, "U.S. Public Diplomacy," pp. 14–15.